3 9082 08332 1748

W9-DGV-031

DATE DUE

APR 1 0 2007

NOV 1 6 **2010**

MAR **2 4** 2011

'OCT 9 2014

Return Material Promptly

27.93   3

LIBYA
in Pictures

Francesca Di Piazza

Twenty-First Century Books

Contents

3 9082 08332 1748

Website address: www.lernerbooks.co

Twenty-First Century Books
A division of Lerner Publishing Group
241 First Avenue North
Minneapolis, MN 55401 U.S.A.

web enhanced @ www.vgsbooks.com

CULTURAL LIFE 48

► Religion. Literature and Communications. Architecture and Art. Music and Dance. Holidays and Festivals. Sports and Recreation. Food.

THE ECONOMY 58

► Oil and Other Mining. Industry and Trade. Agriculture and Fishing. Transportation. Services and Tourism. The Future.

FOR MORE INFORMATION

Library of Congress Cataloging-in-Publication Data

DiPiazza, Francesca, 1961-
     Libya in pictures / by Francesca DiPiazza.
        p.   cm. — (Visual geography series)
     Includes bibliographical references and index.
     ISBN-13: 978-0-8225-2549-3 (lib. bdg. : alk. paper)
     ISBN-10: 0-8225-2549-6 (lib. bdg. : alk. paper)
     1. Libya—Pictorial works—Juvenile literature. 2. Libya—Description and travel—Juvenile literature.
  I. Title. II. Visual geography series (Minneapolis, Minn.)
  DT220.22.D57 2006
  961.2'0022'2—dc22   20050156377

Manufactured in the United States of America
1 2 3 4 5 6 – BP – 11 10 09 08 07 06

INTRODUCTION

The map of Libya shows a slim strip of green along the Mediterranean coastline of North Africa. Little black dots along the coastline mark regularly spaced cities and ports. South of the green strip is a large square—about 90 percent of the area—mostly colored in tan. This is the Sahara Desert. In the entire expanse of tan, only a few black dots mark cities. The area looks empty. An Arab saying states, "The desert is the garden of Allah [God], from which the Lord of the Faithful removed all unnecessary human and animal life, so that there might be one place on earth where he can walk in peace."

But the desert is not altogether empty. Oases, where water comes from underground, are scattered throughout the Sahara. An intriguing array of animals and plants have adapted to extreme heat and lack of water. Camels and date palm trees present a popular image, and they are central to desert life. The fennec, or desert fox, is a less well-known desert resident that displays classic survival skills. This little tan fox sleeps burrowed under the sand during the heat of day and comes out

at night to hunt. The fox gets most of its water from the body fluids of the animals it eats.

Like the desert fox, the humans who have lived in the desert for thousands of years have learned to protect themselves from heat and to fully use every available resource. Wandering desert groups have lived independently, protecting their freedom, for generations. Sheltering in tents and wrapped in veils against the sun and blowing sands, these nomads move frequently with their flocks of animals to find grazing land and water. They rarely eat their animals but use their milk for food. Some peoples raise crops in areas with water access, either natural or through human-made wells and irrigation.

Traveling groups of traders have also crisscrossed the trackless desert for generations. Caravans brought such precious metals as gold, exotic materials, such as ebony and ivory, and human beings to be sold as slaves from the interior of Africa across the desert to the shores of the Mediterranean. They carried back precious salt and manufactured goods.

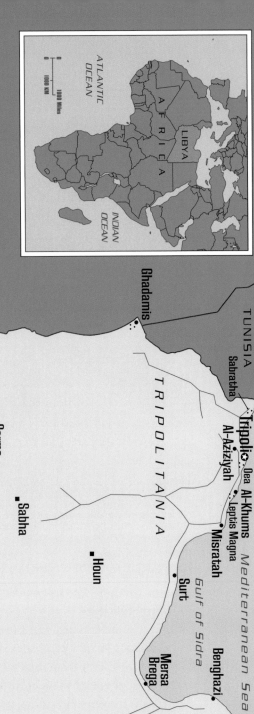

Over the course of history, many different peoples have settled the Mediterranean coast of Libya. Seafaring, trading Phoenicians from the Middle East arrived in about 1300 B.C. The armies, engineers, and farmers of the great Roman Empire made the coast a thriving and fertile land. Greek colonists, too, brought the civilization of the classical world, with its temples and teaching, to North Africa. The most lasting influence in Libya came from the Arab invasions of the seventh century. Libyans mostly call themselves Arabs, a blend of these arrivals from the Arabian Peninsula and the native peoples of Libya. They speak Arabic and practice Islam, the faith the Arabs brought. In the 1500s, the Islamic Ottoman Empire from modern Turkey gained control of the coasts and held the area for a long time—with the help of pirates. Libya's most recent colonizers were the Italians in the twentieth century. All along, the desert peoples had accepted foreign influences and trade. But they resisted foreign rule and gained a reputation as fierce and independent people.

Libya gained its independence from colonial rule in 1951. One of the poorest countries in the world, Libya's main trade resources were esparto grass, used for making fine paper, and leftover scrap metal from armed warfare. But in 1955, oil was discovered under the desert and Libya became potentially one of the richest countries. In 1969 another product of the desert—Colonel Muammar Qadhafi, born in the desert to desert people—overthrew the government. He has ruled Libya ever since, with a sometimes dramatic mix of charisma and ruthless determination. His political tactics led the country into international isolation, especially after the downing of two commercial jetliners in the late 1980s. Libyan agents were accused in both bombings. Qadhafi refused to surrender the suspects, and as a consequence, years of international sanctions against Libya ensued. In the late 1990s and early 2000s, with Libya's economy in shambles, Qadhafi finally met a series of United Nations and U.S. requirements, including release of bombing suspects, and the sanctions were lifted. As a result, Libya is moving back into good relations with the family of nations.

THE LAND

Libya is a nation of mostly arid (extremely dry) lands in North Africa. North Africa is largely covered by the Sahara, the world's largest desert. (*Sahara* is the Arabic word for "desert.") Libya's neighbors are Egypt to the east, Sudan to the southeast, Chad and Niger to the south, Algeria to the west, and Tunisia to the northwest. Italy, Greece, and the islands of Malta lie northward across the Mediterranean Sea.

Libya extends southward from the shores of the Mediterranean Sea into the Sahara, which covers more than 90 percent of the country. Fewer than 10 percent of the Libyan people make their homes in the desert. Most people live in northern cities and towns near the seacoast. The rest of the population lives in scattered villages and desert oases—isolated areas of fertile soil and freshwater springs.

The country's land area totals 679,358 square miles (1,759,537 square kilometers), making Libya slightly larger than Alaska. Libya has two major geographic regions—the Mediterranean Region and the Sahara.

● Mediterranean Region

The Mediterranean Region makes up less than 10 percent of the country. The region is comprised of two coastal lowlands—the Al-Jifarah Plain to the west and the Al-Marj Plain to the east—separated by a narrow section of desert called the Sirte. The coastal plains receive some rain and are fed by irrigation (artificial watering) systems, which allow for the cultivation of crops. Sandy beaches, salt marshes, and shallow lagoons are also found in the lowlands, which are home to most Libyans. Tripoli, Libya's capital, lies in the western part of the Mediterranean Region.

The Al-Jifarah Plain supports hardy shrubs and grasses and is near the border with Tunisia to the west. An important farming zone, the plain spreads southward to the Nafusah Plateau, a long, raised area of limestone that runs from west to east. The plateau reaches an elevation of 2,500 feet (762 meters) above sea level and is too dry for much agriculture.

In the eastern Mediterranean region, the fertile Al-Marj Plain follows the coast as it juts northward and then eastward toward Egypt.

Scrubby vegetation grows along **Libya's rocky coastline.** The Mediterranean Sea keeps the weather there more temperate than in inland areas.

Libya's second-largest city, Benghazi, is on this stretch of coast. To the south of the Al-Marj Plain, forests of pine and juniper trees cover the 3,000-foot (914 m) tall Al-Akhdar Mountains, or Green Mountains. Farther south, stony, tree-covered hills and plateaus of semidesert grasslands give way to the Libyan Desert, part of the Sahara.

The narrow Sirte Desert, which separates the two coastal plains, blends southward from the Gulf of Sidra into the Sahara. In many places, only salt marshes and oil pipelines mark the landscape of the Sirte. This strip of desert has long been a barrier to travel and communication between Libya's western and eastern coast.

⊙ The Sahara

South of the Mediterranean Region sprawls the enormous Sahara, the desert covering more than one-third of Africa. One of the driest areas on earth, the Sahara was once a well-watered grassland. But climatic changes beginning about six thousand years ago gradually turned the region into a sea of gravel and drifting sand, where huge, waterless plateaus lie among mountains of wind-sculpted rock. A few oases dot the Sahara. In these spots, wells have been built, allowing people to grow crops or raise livestock.

The Sahara can be divided into many different sections. In the north, Libya's major oil deposits lie under the desert. In western Libya, the Sahara is mostly uninhabited except for scattered oases. Sabha and Murzuq, two of the largest oases in this area, support nomadic herders as well as settled farmers. These two oases stand between two sand seas—vast expanses of shifting sand dunes—the Awbari Sand Sea to the northwest and the Murzuq Sand Sea to the south.

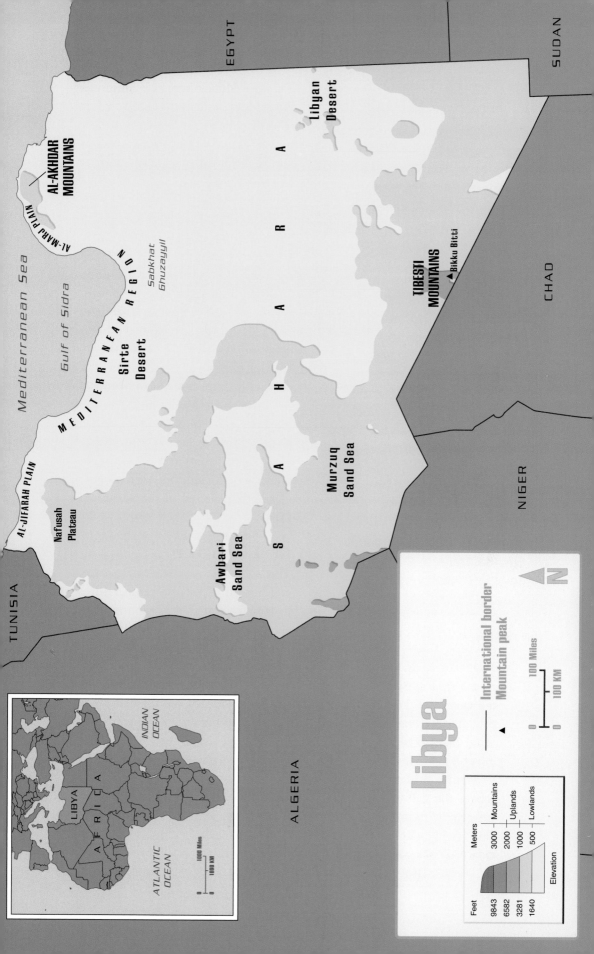

EGYPT

SUDAN

Libyan Desert

AL-AKHDAR MOUNTAINS

AL-MARJ PLAIN

Mediterranean Sea

Gulf of Sidra

MEDITERRANEAN REGION

Sabkhat Ghuzayyil

Sirte Desert

S A H A R A

TIBESTI MOUNTAINS

▲ Bikku Bitti

CHAD

TUNISIA

MEDITERRANEAN PLAIN

AL-JIFARAH PLAIN

Nafusah Plateau

Awbari Sand Sea

Murzuq Sand Sea

NIGER

ALGERIA

AFRICA

LIBYA

INDIAN OCEAN

ATLANTIC OCEAN

1000 Miles
1000 KM

Libya

N

International border
▲ Mountain peak

0   100 Miles
0   100 KM

Elevation

Feet	Meters	
9843	3000	Mountains
6582	2000	Uplands
3281	1000	
1640	500	Lowlands

DEATH IN THE DESERT

It's easy to get lost in the desert. The Sahara is as large as the entire United States and is more than 3 million square miles (7.7 million sq. km) of largely trackless, featureless land. And it's a dangerous place to get lost in. The surface heat of the sand can reach 175°F (79°C). In the extreme heat, one day without water will lead to death. The human body will sweat 24 pints (14 liters) a day. If this water is not replaced, the body starts to draw on the water in its own blood. The blood becomes very thick and is unable to circulate properly and carry away heat. Body heat rises rapidly because it is not being cooled through circulation. Sweating stops and the skin becomes flushed and red. Unless the person is quickly hospitalized, this explosive heat rise quickly leads to death.

The sand dunes here rise hundreds of feet high and are up to 100 miles (160 km) long. Wide highlands of bare rock shaped by wind erosion spread across much of the rest of the western desert.

The desert in southern Libya includes thousands of square miles of tall sand dunes that constantly shift like waves and travel with the desert's prevailing winds. The Tibesti Mountains cross the southern Libyan border into Chad and includes Bikku Bitti, Libya's highest point at 7,436 feet (2,266 m).

Along the country's eastern borders with Egypt and Sudan, south of the Al-Akhdar Mountains, lies the Libyan Desert, a barren, sun-baked plain within the Sahara. Few trails or settlements exist in this immense wilderness. Most of the region's population is centered in the Al-Kufrah Oasis.

◉ Climate

Throughout Libya the climate is dry and hot. In the south, temperatures in January, the coldest month, average 63°F (17°C). Temperatures in July, the hottest month, average 100°F (38°C). In the north, however, steady southern breezes from the Mediterranean Sea help moderate temperatures throughout the year. The coastal city of Tripoli averages 52°F (11°C) in January and 82°F (28°C) in July. But high temperatures in Tripoli and in other coastal Libyan cities often break 110°F (43°C). The highest temperature ever recorded on earth, 136°F (58°C), scorched Al-Aziziyah, a town near Tripoli, in 1922.

Winter ushers in cooler temperatures to the country's mountains, where the soil often freezes. Cold, wet winter air sometimes brings light snow to the plains and highlands of northeastern Libya, a region that receives from 16 to 20 inches (40 to 50 centimeters) of precipitation each year. In fact, the Al-Akhdar Mountains are the wettest part of Libya, with as much as 24 inches (60 cm) of annual rainfall.

Sand dunes of the Sahara sculpted by the wind, are among the most beautiful desert sights. But most of the Sahara is barren, gravel plain.

Benghazi and Tripoli each average 14 inches (36 cm) of precipitation a year. Violent storms sometimes strike the coast in winter and spring.

In the Sahara, temperatures vary greatly from day to night. The blazing daytime sun reflects off the barren ground, radiating heat just above the surface. The lack of cloud cover, which would help retain the heat, causes nighttime temperatures to fall drastically. Thermometer readings in the Sahara often break 100°F (38°C) at midday and then plunge below freezing at night.

The clouds that form over the highlands of northern Libya drop their precipitation before reaching the desert. As a result, most places in the Sahara get less than 4 inches (10 cm) of rain a year, and some villages and oases see no rain for years at a time. The oasis of Sabha, one of the driest places on earth, receives an average of 0.4 inches (1 cm) of rainfall each year. The valleys of the Tibesti Mountains in the south receive slightly more precipitation than the surrounding desert, catching moist air moving north from the equator, which creates some grazing land in the region.

Every five or six years, northern Libya suffers a severe drought (period of little or no rain) that destroys crops and dries up wells. The drought may last from one to two years. Another danger is a fierce, hot, sand-laden wind known as the ghibli (Arabic for "south wind," also called the sirocco). It passes northward across the desert in the spring and autumn. The ghibli's blinding sandstorms kill crops and livestock. This scorching wind brings a sudden, drastic temperature rise and lasts one to four days.

 To find links to more information about the Sahara, visit www.vgsbooks.com.

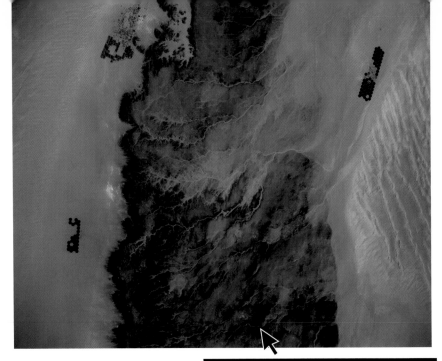

A satellite picture of Libya shows small green circles of irrigated cropland on either side of a mountain range. The desert encroaches from all sides.

Water, Environmental Issues, and Natural Resources

Water is Libya's greatest environmental concern. The country has no permanent rivers, no freshwater lakes, and little dependable rainfall. Water in the marshes near the seacoast is too salty for use. The streams in the northern highlands run only during rainy seasons. Sudden, brief storms sometimes fill and overflow wadis (dry streambeds), causing flash floods that can damage crops and buildings. Much of the rain in the desert quickly evaporates in the heat.

During the prehistoric period, when abundant rain fell in the Sahara, aquifers (natural underground sources of water) filled with water. Libya taps this water through wells for most of its freshwater supply. But it is a nonrenewable resource: in modern times, not enough rain falls to refill the aquifers.

The growth of agriculture and population has worsened the country's water problems. Irrigation projects that draw water for crops from the underground reserves have depleted the wells that many towns rely on for drinking water. In addition, when aquifers run low, the remaining water comes into contact with natural salts in the sand and rocks through which the water passes. This leaves the water too salty for drinking or for crops. In a process called desertification, these stresses, drought, and the overuse of dry land turn them into barren desert.

In an attempt to bring more water to the north for people and agriculture, the Libyan government began the Great Man Made River (GMR) project in 1984, a five-phase project to be completed in 2034.

This system of pumps, canals, and reservoirs links desert wells to coastal regions. Tripoli began receiving water from the GMR in 1996. This is the world's largest water development project and, at a cost of $25 billion, the most expensive. But the GMR also threatens the livelihood of the desert's nomadic herders, who depend on the wells for themselves and their livestock. Some scientists believe that the GMR could empty the aquifers by 2070. The results could have serious implications for wildlife, agriculture, and human life in Libya.

Desalination plants provide an additional source of freshwater. These are plants that desalt, or remove salt, from salt water. Libya began building desalination plants near major cities in the 1980s, and an expansion program is under way in the 2000s.

Petroleum is Libya's main natural resource. The nation's enormous reserves of petroleum are the largest in Africa and among the largest in the world. Libya relies entirely on this fossil fuel for its power and most of its income. But oil removal damages the desert environment, and oil spills from tankers damage coastal waters. As oil is also a nonrenewable resource, the country is challenged to find alternate sources for the future. Solar energy (power from the sun) is a safe, renewable resource. In the twenty-first century, some buildings have been constructed with solar panels to harness this energy. Libya also seeks to develop nuclear power as a source of energy. While nuclear power plants produce a clean form of energy, they also create dangerous radioactive waste.

Natural gas is another important resource. The country also has deposits of iron ore—an important ingredient of steel—as well as potash (used in fertilizer), coal, gypsum, and manganese. Sea salt is gathered from the lagoons and depressions along the Mediterranean coast. Natron, a hardened form of salt, is collected for use in oil refining, soap making, and water purification. (Ancient Egyptians used natron to make mummies.) Limestone, granite, and marble quarries supply the country's busy construction industry.

Flora and Fauna

Despite Libya's harsh climate, only a few places in the desert have no plant life. A variety of vegetation has adapted to dry conditions. Many varieties of cacti, including the edible prickly pear, thrive throughout the country. Deep root systems, such as the roots of low, thorny acacia trees, can reach underground moisture. To limit the amount of water lost to evaporation, plants reduce the surface area of their leaves, which become thick and small. Some plants store water in underground bulbs. Hardy seeds from short, spiky grasses can survive for years in the dry ground. When it rains, the desert briefly comes alive with green as dormant seeds sprout.

A bather enjoys a cool moment in a waterfall fed by Libya's occasional rains. Brush grow alongside the waterfall.

In some highlands of the Sahara, wild olive and cypress trees—some of them thousands of years old—survive on sparsely watered hillsides. Esparto grass, once a principal export, is still gathered for its tough fiber, which is made into rope and paper. In oases, date palms stand tall, providing a staple food as well as fiber and building material. Fig trees, oleander trees, and henna shrubs, used for dye, also grow in oases.

Mediterranean flora thrives along Libya's coast, with large areas of cultivated olive and citrus fruit trees. Lilies, narcissus, and lotus flowers bloom in the valleys of the Al-Akhdar Mountains, where underground streams also water tough juniper and cypress trees. Libya has carried out several forestation and desert reclamation programs, planting millions of eucalyptus, acacia, cypress, and cedar trees in the highlands and plains of the north. These have not flourished, due to the climate.

Animals that live in Libya have adapted to the hot, dry environment. Light colors reflect sunlight, so many desert animals are pale, sandy colors. These colors also provide camouflage protection from predators such as hyenas, wildcats, and jackals. Many desert animals are nocturnal, or active at night. They avoid the heat of the day by sleeping in holes or burrows in the sand. The temperature 3 feet (9 m) below the desert surface stays a steady 75°F (24°C), day and night. Desert hedgehogs have large ears that help them stay cool. Blood circulates through their thin-skinned ears and releases body heat. Nocturnal, buff-colored fennecs (the smallest kind of fox) also have large,

Fennec

batlike ears. Fennecs and many other desert predators get most of their water from the body fluids of the animals they eat. The addax, a small antelope with black, spiral horns, never drinks water at all but gets all its moisture from grasses. These and other antelopes and gazelles have been hunted nearly to extinction for their skins and beautiful horns.

Domesticated camels, originally from Asia, were introduced to Libya about two thousand years ago and are well suited to desert life. Long eyelashes and heavy eyebrows protect their eyes. Wide, padded feet can tolerate hot sands and give the great beasts stability on loose sands, like snowshoes give on snow. Camels can eat almost any kind of plants, even thorny ones. They can go for days without food and weeks without water.

Desert lizards, such as skinks, and snakes also survive by burrowing underneath the sand during the day. Libyan desert dwellers watch carefully for scorpions and poisonous snakes such as adders and vipers. Insects include butterflies, ants, locusts, and several kinds of beetles, including the dung beetle. Camel spiders grow up to 5 inches (12 cm) long and hunt insects or even small lizards, birds, and rodents.

A well-known desert rodent, the jerboa, uses its long back legs to leap over hot ground. Its tail, about 6 inches (15 cm) long, is as long as its body. Jerboas are favorite prey of hawks and eagles, which nest in the dry highlands of the south. Vultures also fly over the desert, while gulls, terns, and ducks favor the salty marshes of the coastal regions. Each winter millions of birds migrate southward across the Mediterranean Sea on their way to tropical Africa, many of them flying for forty hours without stopping over 1,000 miles (1,609 km) across the Sahara. Libya sees warblers, swallows, nightingales, herons, and more migratory birds passing through.

AN ANCIENT HUNTING DOG

The sloughi is a sight hound, a dog that relies on its keen vision to hunt prey in the open desert landscape. This fast and beautiful dog is native to Libya and other parts of North Africa. Representations of sight-houndlike dogs resembling the sloughi go back to ancient Egypt. The desert-dwelling Berbers and Bedouin peoples highly treasured the sloughi's great hunting skills, elegance, and loyalty. By the twenty-first century, the dog has become a very uncommon breed. For links to more information about the sloughi, visit www.vgsbooks.com.

Cities

Libya's main cities cluster near the Mediterranean coast, where most of the country's agriculture and industry also are concentrated. About

"THE WHITE CITY"

In hot climates, people paint buildings light colors to reflect the sun and keep them cool. Tripoli has many white buildings that glare in the bright light. In 1307 an Arab traveler, At Tigiani, described arriving at the city: "When we approached, we were blinded by the brilliant whiteness of the city from which the burning rays of the sun were reflected. I was convinced that rightly is Tripoli called the White City."

90 percent of Libya's 5.6 million people live in urban areas. Tripoli lies on the western part of Libya's coastline. Benghazi is across the Sirte Desert on the eastern shore.

TRIPOLI Libya's capital since 1951, Tripoli has 1.2 million residents—one-fifth of the country's population. The capital is also Libya's busiest port and main manufacturing and transportation center.

Tripoli's harbor has long been an important center of trade. Phoenician traders from the Middle East first settled the site nearly three thousand years ago. Tripoli was the destination of caravans that linked the coast with trading centers far to the south. When the region fell under Roman control in the first century B.C., the city became the seat of a wealthy and fertile province. The spread of Islam and later Ottoman rule brought Arab and Turkish culture and the architecture of the mosque (Islamic house of prayer) to the city. In the early

Cars and pedestrians jam the streets of **Tripoli's medina, or old city.** Vendors sell all kinds of goods along the sidewalks. To learn more about Tripoli and Libya's other cities, visit www.vgsbooks.com for links.

twentieth century, Italian rulers expanded the city, adding wide boulevards, office and apartment buildings, parks, and small factories. During the first oil boom of the 1960s, new high-rises and factories appeared on the city's outskirts as thousands of newcomers arrived to find work. In the twenty-first century, Tripoli is a sophisticated city adapted to modern life, with Internet cafés, air-conditioning, health clubs, satellite TV, and even plans for a water park.

Tripoli's medina (Arabic for "town") is the old center of the city, with narrow, winding streets and small, neighborhood mosques. Here people crowd the souk, or open-air market, where vendors sell many sorts of foods, spices, clothing, and other goods.

Tripoli's major industries include oil refining, textile manufacturing, food processing, and the making of handicrafts such as carpets and leatherwork. The city also is home to the world-class Jamahiriya Museum, which exhibits artifacts from every era of Libya's history.

SECONDARY CITIES Benghazi (population 1 million) is the nation's second-largest city and the main port of northeastern Libya. It is named after ibn Ghazi, a local holy man of the 1400s. Lying along the Gulf of Sidra, Benghazi is a center for oil production and refining. Benghazi's busy port also hosts cargo ships that bring foreign imports to Libya. The ancient Greeks founded a port city here in the 630s B.C. Later, under Turkish rule, the city was the administrative center of the Ottoman province of Cyrenaica. The city changed hands several times during World War II (1939–1945), when German, Italian, and British forces fought fierce desert battles for control of Cyrenaica. Benghazi became the seat of Libya's first university in 1955.

Misratah (population 170,000), on the western coast of the Gulf of Sidra, is Libya's third-largest city. The historic center of the town was once a gathering point for caravans from central Africa. In the twenty-first century, Misratah maintains one of the oldest carpet industries in Libya, but much of the city's prosperity comes from a local steel mill.

Tobruk (population 140,000) is on the northeastern coast near the Egyptian border. It is famous as the site of some of the most important World War II battles in North Africa. World War II cemeteries attract tourists, but the city is otherwise a plain harbor town.

Sabha (population 75,000) is the largest oasis in Libya. Irrigation canals also supply the area with freshwater for crops. An ancient center of Libya's caravan trade, Sabha marks a junction of two major trails linking the coast to the interior of Africa. Heavy trucks deposit and collect cargo at Sabha, but camels still provide dependable means of transportation on unpaved routes through the desert.

HISTORY AND GOVERNMENT

The earliest evidence of human settlements in Libya dates to more than ten thousand years ago. Hunter-gatherers moved across lush grasslands in the south, where they hunted large herds of giraffes, elephants, and antelope. These prehistoric people left a record of their way of life by carving and painting on rock walls.

Over the centuries, Libya has seen many different peoples cross its lands in search of cropland and pasture for their herds. One such group called itself the Imazighan, or "free people" (later called Berbers). The Imazighan arrived from southwestern Asia sometime after 3000 B.C. and gradually spread across North Africa.

At the same time, North Africa was in the middle of a climate change. Rainfall was decreasing, and the topsoil of the region gradually turned to infertile sand. No longer able to grow crops, farmers became nomadic herders. Nomads travel in search of water and grazing land for their herds of sheep and goats. Some nomads used horses and horse-drawn chariots and began trading. In dry years when food ran short, some nomads raided the small coastal settlements along the Mediterranean as well as the desert oases that were gradually becoming centers of trade and agriculture.

For centuries, the Imazighan also made raids into Egypt. The Egyptians knew these peoples as the Levu, or Libyans, and gave the name Libya to the region where they lived.

Phoenician and Greek Settlement

In about 1300 B.C., Phoenicians—seafaring, trading people from present-day Lebanon—began building settlements along the coast of North Africa for trade. Imazighan caravans brought ivory, gold, and slaves—men, women, and children forced to walk across the Sahara—from the African interior and traded them to the Phoenicians in exchange for imports from other Mediterranean ports. The Phoenician towns of Oea, Leptis Magna, and Sabratha—known as Tripolis (three cities)—grew along natural harbors of the coast. The area surrounding these cities became known as Tripolitania. Their culture and language was called Punic, from "Phoenician." Busy trade made Tripolitania wealthy and powerful.

At the same time, the Greeks of southeastern Europe were founding colonies in eastern Libya in a region known as Cyrenaica, which took its name from the Greek settlement of Cyrene. In 631 B.C., Greek immigrants established Euhesperides (modern Benghazi). These cities thrived as trade and agriculture flourished in the region. The bustling city of Cyrene became the site of a medical school and a well-known Greek academy.

Far to the southwest, in an area called Fezzan, an Imazighan people known as the Garamantes were building their capital at the oasis of Germa. Archaeologists have found elaborate tombs and ruins in Germa, where the Garamantes controlled the busy caravan trade between central Africa and Tripolitania. They traded salt, a highly valuable food preservative, for goods from the interior.

◉ Romans Arrive

Carthage (a Punic city near modern Tunis, Tunisia) faced a strong rival in Rome, a republic based across the Mediterranean on the Italian Peninsula. In the third century B.C., Carthage and Rome fought the Punic Wars. This series of clashes ended with a Roman victory in 146 B.C.

In 46 B.C., the Roman emperor Julius Caesar annexed (took over) Cyrenaica as well as Tripolitania and established the Roman province of Africa Nova (New Africa). To protect Africa Nova from enemies in the south, the Romans constructed a chain of forts. Roman engineers also built extensive irrigation networks, and

The ruins of an **ancient Roman amphitheater** still stand in the Roman town of Leptis Magna in Libya. For links to more information about Leptis Magna, visit www.vgsbooks.com

Roman settlers cleared vast acreages in Tripolitania. Using local laborers and African slaves, the Roman estates supplied the empire with huge crops of grain, wine, and olive oil. The Romans also linked Roman towns with new roads. Latin, the language of the Romans, and other aspects of Roman culture—including art, architecture, and religion—took hold. But the Romans found that they could not subdue the Imazighan, whom they and the Greeks called Berbers, from a word meaning "barbarian."

Caravans brought valuable trade goods such as gold, ivory, ebony, peacock and ostrich feathers, and human beings. Traders also sold wild animals to entertain the Romans in their circuses (public shows). Goods transported southward through the Sahara included grain, wine, and manufactured goods such as cloth, pottery, and glass. Trade increased with the introduction of the camel, which became the best means of transporting goods across the desert. Caravans engaged in the salt trade—carrying salt from the north into the interior of the continent—sometimes used thousands of camels.

Division and Fall of the Roman Empire

By the fourth century, the people of Africa Nova were adopting a new religion from the Middle East—Christianity. Although most Romans accepted the faith, most Berbers did not.

Conflict within the Roman Empire brought a division of the empire in 395. The Western Roman Empire, with its capital in Rome, took control of western Libya. Eastern Libya was ruled by the Byzantine (Eastern Roman) Empire, with its capital in Constantinople (modern Istanbul, Turkey).

The Romans had never conquered most Berbers, who still traveled freely among the oases of the south. Berber groups formed confederations that governed the Saharan peoples. In the fifth century, with the Roman Empire divided and weakened, the Berbers allied with the Vandals, a Germanic group from northern Europe.

The Vandals conquered Roman Libya in 431 and destroyed much of Roman culture there. After making North Africa their base, the Vandals overran the Roman cities of southern Europe. Unable to withstand these attacks, the Western Roman Empire collapsed in 476. The Byzantine Empire remained in control of eastern Libya. The Vandals were better warriors than administrators, and in the 500s, the Byzantines drove the Vandals out. They took over Libya but soon proved to be inefficient rulers themselves.

By the seventh century, Berber and other native groups had established their own kingdoms and were gaining control over parts of Cyrenaica and Tripolitania. Berber rebellions and poor Byzantine administration left Libya open to new invasions and new influences.

The Coming of Islam

One of these new influences was Islam, a faith introduced by the Prophet (spiritual spokesperson) Muhammad on the Arabian Peninsula in the early seventh century. According to Islam, God's will was set forth in the Quran, the Islamic holy book. Among Muhammad's followers, called Muslims, the Quran became the basis for a new code of civil law known as sharia.

By 644 Arab Muslim forces had driven the Byzantine armies from their strongholds and gained control of Libya. In cities along the North African coast, Arabs emerged as merchants and officials. Arabic became the most common language. Arab merchants gradually took control of trans-Saharan commerce and spread Islam along the caravan routes that reached southward through Fezzan. Berbers accepted the Islamic faith and adapted it to fit with their traditions, but they continued to resist any foreign control.

Many conflicts divided the Muslims. Islam split into Sunni and Shiite branches. Sunni Muslims supported the election of Arab nobles to the caliphate (seat of Islamic leadership). Shiite Muslims believed in leadership only by caliphs who were descendants of Muhammad's family. These divisions within the religion led to further conflict in North Africa. Over the next two centuries, different Islamic dynasties (families of rulers) fought for control.

In the eleventh century, two powerful Arab clans, known as the Bedouin, invaded North Africa. The Bedouin subdued and gradually intermarried with many of the Berbers. The clan divisions and family groups they established remained the most important social divisions in Libya into the twentieth century.

Spaniards, Ottomans, and Pirates

By 1500 the rising power of Christian nations in Europe began to threaten Tripolitania. In 1510 a Spanish army attacked and looted Tripoli. In 1524 Charles I, the king of Spain, turned the city over to the Knights of Saint John, a Christian military brotherhood that was fighting against Islamic control of the Mediterranean.

To counter European attacks, Muslim leaders strengthened the major port cities along the African Mediterranean coast. This region—called the Barbary Coast—became the base for continuous raids, attacks, and lootings by rival corsairs, or government-approved pirates, from North Africa. From Algeria, for example, Khayr al-Din—also known as Barbarossa (Red Beard)—launched raids on European ships in the Mediterranean. Barbarossa controlled much of western North Africa and declared the territory part of the Ottoman Empire, a Muslim realm based in modern Turkey.

In 1551 an Ottoman fleet of corsairs captured Tripoli from the Knights of Saint John. The busy harbor of Tripoli and the surrounding area became an Ottoman province.

Under Ottoman rule, Tripoli remained an important market for goods brought by caravan from the Sahara and central Africa. But the city's main business became the trade in stolen goods and hostages taken by corsairs. These corsairs, who sailed from ports all along the Barbary Coast, turned over part of their profits to the Ottoman rulers. European nations paid regular tributes to Tripoli's rulers for the safe passage of European ships through Mediterranean waters.

By the late seventeenth century, political struggles among the rulers of Tripoli were weakening the hold of the Ottoman Empire over the Barbary Coast. In 1711 Ahmed Karamanli, the son of a Turkish officer and a

PIRATE SHIPS

Originally, pirates on the Barbary Coast used ships called galleys—ships propelled by oars. Up to 150 human rowers powered fifty banks of oars. The 150-foot (46 m) ships also had one square sail. A ram, or heavy, pointed beak, was mounted on the prow (front) of the ship, for piercing victim ships. Other weapons included culverins (slim, maneuverable cannons) and other cannons. Sophisticated sailing ships with multipart sails began to replace galleys in the mid-seventeenth century. These ships required smaller crews, had more space for cargo, and were faster.

An illustration from 1846 depicts the **U.S. bombing of Tripoli,** which occurred in 1805.

Libyan woman, seized power and founded the Karamanli dynasty. He ruled as an independent tyrant within the Ottoman Empire.

As Mediterranean trade increased, European and North American merchants became less willing to pay the pirates for safe passage. In 1801 ruler Yusuf Karamanli tried to make the United States pay an annual sum of $250,000. In return, the U.S. Navy blockaded Tripoli. The Libyans captured the warship the USS *Philadelphia* and took the crew prisoner. Four years later, in 1805, a force of U.S. Marines successfully attacked by land and captured the town. Because of military action, Barbary Coast piracy gradually came to an end. In 1811 the Ottoman Empire regained direct control of Libya and ended the Karamanli dynasty.

The Sanusi Brotherhood

In the 1830s, the Islamic scholar and holy man Sidi Muhammad Ali al-Sanusi (known as the Grand Sanusi) came to Libya. He was a Sufi, a member of an Islamic mystical sect, and a scholar of the Quran. Al-Sanusi organized the Sanusi Brotherhood. This Muslim religious and social reform group claimed that all educated Muslims had the right to interpret the sacred teachings for themselves. The Grand Sanusi eventually settled in the highlands of the Al-Akhdar Mountains, where he founded a series of holy lodges. These lodges functioned as monasteries, schools, courts, and places of pilgrimage for the members of the Sanusi Brotherhood.

Gradually, the Sanusis brought unity to the many feuding clans of the desert, who liked the independent-minded group. They organized an effective resistance to the Ottoman Turks and to European colonial powers who had begun occupying many parts of Africa. The Sanusi headquarters moved to the Al-Kufrah Oasis, which became a hub of guerrillas (small, independent groups of fighters) resisting foreign control, including British control of neighboring Sudan and Egypt.

Italian Colonization

Italy was a latecomer to the European colonial powers' "scramble for Africa." In the late nineteenth century, archaeologists uncovered Roman ruins in the sands of northern Libya. This event prompted many Italian leaders to claim that Libya, as an ancient Roman province, belonged under Italian rule. In 1911 Italian forces captured Tripoli. Ottoman power in the Mediterranean was weak, and the empire soon recognized the independence of Cyrenaica and Tripolitania. Italy then brought these regions under Italian rule.

Despite Sanusi guerrilla resistance inland, Italy remained in control of the growing cities and farmland of the coast. The Italian government began moving Italian farmers into Tripolitania to relieve unemployment and social unrest within Italy, forcing Libyans to move from their land.

When World War I (1914–1918) began in Europe, the Sanusis sided with the Ottomans and Germans against Italy and Great Britain, known as the Allies, in the war. Sanusi fighters attacked British forces in Egypt, still under British control. Libyans began calling for self-rule. Britain agreed to a truce with the Sanusi leader, Sidi Muhammad Idris al-Sanusi, and recognized him as the emir (Islamic ruler) of Cyrenaica.

World War I ended with an Allied victory. Italy, under the dictatorship of Mussolini, moved to crush Libyan resistance to Italian occupation. In 1922 leaders of a Libyan nationalist movement (a group working for a unified and independent country) proposed that Idris

THE END OF THE GREAT CARAVANS

By the twentieth century, the large caravan trade was dying out. Caravans, at the peak of trans-Sahara trade, had been convoys of sometimes thousands of camels. About 1905 U.S. writer and traveler Mabel Loomis Todd, in her book *Tripoli the Mysterious*, described seeing a caravan of 250 camels entering Tripoli after ten months in the desert:

"The camels stepped slowly, heavily laden with huge bales securely tied up—ivory and gold dust, skins and feathers. Wrapped in dingy drapery and carrying guns ten feet long, . . . Bedouins led the weary camels across the sun-baked square. In the . . . silent company marched a few genuine Tuaregs, black veils strapped lightly over their faces and enshrouded in black or dark brown wraps. . . . All were ragged beyond belief."

become emir of Tripolitania and Cyrenaica. Although he accepted, Idris soon fled to Egypt to avoid being captured by the Italians.

Guerrilla War

After its defeat in World War I, the Ottoman Empire collapsed and was replaced by the Turkish Republic. In 1923 Turkey surrendered its former Ottoman territories, which the Allies divided among themselves. Italy laid formal claim to Libya. But in Libya, guerrilla warfare against Italy's oppressive rule continued. Bedouin Sanusi scholar Omar al-Mukhtar became a national resistance leader. Al-Mukhtar organized hit-and-run attacks carried out by his Bedouin followers, who escaped into the desert after raiding ports and settlements along the coast.

The Italians carried on a bloody campaign to defeat the Sanusi guerrillas and to destroy their support among the Bedouin. The regime set up a barbed-wire barrier along the Egyptian border to prevent guerrillas from crossing into Egypt for supplies. By blocking wells, killing livestock, and destroying pasture, the Italians forced many Bedouin into exile. To end local support of the guerrillas, Italians also put 100,000 people in concentration camps, where thousands died of illness and starvation. Their grazing lands were turned over to Italian farmers.

During the 1920s and 1930s, Italy built new roads and railroads, irrigation works, apartment and office buildings, and port facilities in Libya for the Italians' benefit. Thousands of Italian settlers arrived, while many Libyans lost their lands and lived in poverty.

In 1931 the Italian colonial government captured Omar al-Mukhtar and executed the seventy-three-year-old man in a public square in

Italian colonial officials in Libya provided **Italian immigrants** with new housing developments and issued mules, carts, and furniture to the settlers.

Benghazi. Al-Mukhtar's death ended most Sanusi resistance. In 1939 Italy annexed Libya, placing it under total direct rule for the first time. An estimated one-quarter of Libya's population had died in the three decades of Italian occupation.

World War II and Independence

In September 1939, Germany attacked Poland, sparking World War II. Britain and France, the United States, and other countries, known as the Allies, fought against Germany, Italy, and Japan, known as the Axis.

The conflict eventually spread to European colonial holdings in North Africa, and once again, Libya was a battlefield. Idris joined his forces with those of Britain, which still held Egypt as a colony, and Libyan volunteers joined British units fighting in North Africa.

German and British troops fought fiercely against each other in the deserts of Cyrenaica until early 1942. By October British forces had defeated the Axis in North Africa and were occupying Libya.

The fighting had destroyed towns and farms and had driven thousands of refugees from Cyrenaica. Extremely poor and sparsely populated, Libya remained under British military administration until the end of the war in 1945, when the Axis powers were defeated.

In 1947 the United Nations (UN) formed a series of committees to decide Libya's future as a united and independent nation. Libya's independence officially took effect on December 24, 1951.

Sidi Muhammad Idris al-Sanusi became king of Libya. The new king outlawed political parties. To promote the Libyan economy, King

On December 24, 1951, **King Idris I** addressed his fellow citizens as Libya officially celebrated its independence.

Idris maintained friendly relations with UN member nations, especially the United States and Britain. Both countries contributed money to Libya for industrial development. In return, Idris allowed the two nations to build military bases along the Mediterranean coast. This angered many Libyans, who believed these arrangements kept their country under the influence of foreign powers.

Oil and Revolution

In 1959 engineers discovered large reserves of underground oil in Cyrenaica, and several foreign drilling companies rushed in to build wells. The Libyan government received 50 percent of the oil profits, and Libya went from being one of the poorest countries in the world to one of the richest. The government planned new social services and construction projects with the oil income.

Although money was flowing into Libya, much of it financed Idris's large and inefficient government. Idris began to lose popularity as his government failed to implement development plans in Libya. In addition, Idris did little to ally with other Arab Muslim nations, with which many Libyans felt linked politically and spiritually.

Within the small Libyan army, Colonel Muammar Qadhafi, a charismatic young man from a poor Bedouin family, led a group dedicated to overthrowing the Libyan monarchy. Driven by the goal of a single, united Arab nation, Qadhafi planned for the end of all foreign interests in the Arab world.

Qadhafi formed the Revolutionary Command Council (RCC) to take over the Libyan government. On September 1, 1969, while Idris was out of the country, twenty-seven-year-old Qadhafi and his supporters seized government and military buildings in Tripoli and Benghazi. Libyan civilians and members of the military put up little resistance to the coup (sudden, forceful takeover) of the unpopular monarchy.

Libya under Qadhafi

The twelve-member RCC established the Socialist Libyan Arab Republic with Qadhafi as leader and head of the armed forces. The RCC abolished the monarchy and the national legislature and named itself as the new governing organization. It promised to modernize the country and to work for social justice and a fair distribution of oil wealth among all citizens. The new government also pledged to support the cause of Arab unity. This included supporting the Palestinian Arab efforts to reclaim land from the Jewish state of Israel, founded after World War II.

Under Qadhafi the RCC turned Libya into a Socialist state based on sharia. In a Socialist state, the government controls the means of production and distribution of goods. The new government created state-owned enterprises managed by committees of workers. Qadhafi called for direct citizen rule through the establishment of "committees everywhere." He also nationalized, or put under state control, mosques and Islamic lodges and banned the Sanusi order, to enforce greater loyalty to his regime. All political parties remained outlawed, except for the Arab Socialist Union, which supported RCC goals. In addition, Qadhafi seized foreign oil operations in Libya and placed them under government control. The RCC also expelled all Jews and Italians from the country, and their property was confiscated. The new leader closed U.S. and British military bases. By the 1970s, the United States and most European nations had ended diplomatic relations with Libya. True to their aims, the RCC spent massive amounts of money on development projects to improve Libyan standards of living and worked for the social equality of all citizens.

Libya's government spearheaded a cultural revolution in the early 1970s, with the goal of further transforming Libya into a purely Arab, Socialist state. Sharia was strictly enforced. Arabic was declared the nation's official language, and the government banned nightclubs, the use of alcohol, and certain books. The RCC took control of radio and television stations, newspapers, and other forms of communication. Opponents of the Qadhafi regime were jailed, sentenced to death, or forced into exile, and Qadhafi ruled with absolute power. He renamed the country the Great Socialist People's Libyan Arab Jamahiriya.

QADHAFI'S FIRST ADDRESS TO THE "SONS OF THE DESERT"

The Libyan radio station broadcast this announcement from Colonel Qadhafi on September 1, 1969, the day of his revolutionary takeover:

"Your armed forces have toppled the reactionary, backward and corrupt regime. . . . With one strike, your heroic Army has toppled idols and destroyed them in one of Providence's fateful moments. . . . As of now Libya shall be free and sovereign. A republic under the name of the Libyan Arab Republic. . . . No oppressed, or deceived or wronged, no master and no slave; but free brothers in a society over which, God willing, shall flutter the banner of brotherhood and equality. . . . And thus shall we build glory, revive heritage and avenge a wounded dignity. . . . Sons of the Bedouins, sons of the desert, sons of the ancient cities, sons of the countryside, sons of the villages, the hour of work has struck and so let us forge ahead."

A relaxed **Muammar Qadhafi** *(center)* **meets with Libyan students in Tripoli** **in 1973. The charismatic, young leader enjoyed great popular support.**

Some of the changes made by Qadhafi distanced Libyan society from Islamic traditions, and Qadhafi was not popular with fundamentalist Muslims. Women in Libya, for instance, began to enjoy equal status with men in the 1970s—uncommon among Arab nations. The RCC expanded woman's rights in marriage and divorce. Women were encouraged to attend school and were permitted to get jobs.

Qadhafi also began working with other Arab nations to create a pan- (union of all) Arab federation, but none of his efforts succeeded. Relations between Egypt and Libya eventually grew hostile.

Many leaders of other Arab nations also distanced themselves, believing Qadhafi was an unpredictable leader who encouraged revolutionary groups to overthrow their conservative governments. For example, after sending troops to occupy the Aozou Strip, a mineral-rich territory lying along Libya's border with Chad, Qadhafi sent money, equipment, and troops to antigovernment rebels in northern Chad. Libya was also accused of contributing money, weapons, training, and explosives to support terrorist groups fighting against foreign control around the world. This included supporting the Palestine Liberation Organization (PLO) fighting against Israel and the Irish Republican Army (IRA) fighting against British rule in Northern Ireland.

◗ Rising Tensions

Tensions with Europe and the United States worsened in the 1980s. After a series of terrorist incidents in Europe, including PLO attacks in Rome and Vienna, were linked to Qadhafi, the U.S. government

Palestinian leader Yasser Arafat *(left)* and Qadhafi *(right)* enjoy a smile together during a meeting of Arab leaders in 1977 as part of Qadhafi's effort to create an all-Arab federation. Qadhafi has been criticized for supporting organizations that use terrorist tactics, such as the PLO.

imposed economic sanctions (restrictions) on Libya and sent naval forces into the Gulf of Sidra to defy Libya's claim to these waters.

Pressures inside Libya mounted as well. Libyan exiles, with support inside the country, attempted a coup in May 1984. Its failure led to the imprisonment and interrogation of thousands and the execution of an unknown number of people. Government-sponsored assassination squads set out to murder Libyan exiles opposed to Qadhafi.

On April 5, 1986, a bomb in a Berlin nightclub killed two people, including a U.S. serviceman. Convinced Libya was responsible, U.S. bombers attacked Qadhafi's headquarters near Tripoli. About 130 people were killed, including Qadhafi's young adopted daughter. In 1988 Libyan agents were accused of placing a bomb on Pan Am jetliner 103, which exploded over Lockerbie, Scotland, killing 270 people, as well as bombing a French airplane over Niger in 1989, killing 170 people. Qadhafi refused to surrender for trial the suspects in these bomb attacks. In response, the UN imposed economic sanctions on Libya. The restrictions included a ban on international flights in and out of the country and a halt to the sale of military equipment to Libya. The UN toughened the sanctions in 1992, preventing Libya from accessing its money in foreign bank accounts and stopping some sales of oil-production equipment.

As a result, Libya's oil-producing facilities began to deteriorate. In addition, a drop in the world price of oil further damaged the Libyan economy. Meanwhile, some Libyans—within and outside of the country—

demonstrated increasing resistance to the Qadhafi regime. Islamic fundamentalists, calling for a return to their version of early Islam, also opposed Qadhafi's regime. Qadhafi repressed these opponents with arrests, imprisonment, torture, and executions. Suspected opponents and possible rivals in the military were replaced with loyal supporters. To the public, Qadhafi blamed international sanctions for the country's problems, such as a shortage of consumer goods, and he remained popular among a large segment of Libyan society.

Following a 1998 Arab League meeting in which Arab states decided not to challenge UN sanctions, Qadhafi announced that he was turning his back on his ideals for Arab unity. Libya sought instead to develop its relations with sub-Saharan Africa (countries south of the Sahara). Libya became involved in several troubled African countries, including Sudan, Somalia, and Ethiopia, all countries torn by civil war. Qadhafi used Libya's resources to support various African leaders, including Nelson Mandela, the hero of South Africa's struggle for racial justice. Qadhafi has proposed a borderless "United States of Africa" to change the continent into a single nation-state ruled by a single government. His proposals have met with little interest. However, his ideas do raise the possibility of a future pan-African arrangement—like the European Union—for shared economic and peacekeeping efforts.

◉ The End of Sanctions

As sanctions and international isolation continued to take their economic and political toll, Libya began to address its problems. Qadhafi began to make some domestic reforms. The government freed many

Rescue workers comb the **wreckage of Pan Am flight 103,** which was targeted by terrorists over Lockerbie, Scotland. The Libyan government was linked to the attack. The bombing led to years of tension between Libya and the United States.

In October 1997, **South African president Nelson Mandela** *(left)* **and Qadhafi** *(right)* salute a crowd in Libya during a ceremony to present Qadhafi with the award of the Order of Good Hope, South Africa's highest honor awarded to foreign figures.

political prisoners and eased restrictions on foreign travel by Libyans. Private businesses once again were allowed to operate.

Qadhafi began to reform his international standing too. In 1999 Libya met the first of the UN's requirements for lifting sanctions, surrendering the two Libyans suspected in the Pan Am bombing for trial. One was found guilty, and the other was not.

Also in 1999, the Italian government formally apologized to Libya for its violent colonial rule. Italy agreed to pay millions of dollars in compensation for the occupation.

On September 11, 2001, Arab terrorists—supported by Osama bin Laden's fundamentalist Islamic group al-Qaeda—attacked New York City and the Washington, D.C., area. Qadhafi immediately condemned these attacks. He pointed out that he had long opposed fundamentalist groups, which were a threat to his own rule. Libya had put out a warrant for bin Laden's arrest six years earlier. As part of its post-September 11 war on terrorism, the United States led an invasion of Iraq to remove Iraqi president Saddam Hussein, who was mistakenly thought to have weapons of mass destruction (WMD). This war pushed Qadhafi to secretly negotiate with the United States and Great Britain the voluntary end of Libya's plans to develop WMD.

In September 2003, UN sanctions on Libya were lifted after Libya met the remaining UN requirements. These included paying millions of dollars to each of the Pam-Am bombing victims' families. The United States kept its separate sanctions in place, however.

In December 2003, Libya announced it would end its programs to develop WMD as well as chemical and biological weapons. In response, the United States ended years of economic sanctions in September 2004. Libya appears to have ended its support for international terrorism. Also in 2004, Amnesty International, a human rights organization, was given access to Libya for the first time in fifteen years. Amnesty officials shared their findings of serious human rights violations with Qadhafi and made recommendations for changes, including the release of political prisoners. That same year, evidence emerged that Libyan government officials had been part of a 2003 plot to assassinate Crown Prince Abdallah of Saudi Arabia. In 2005 the Libyan government announced plans to bring the country fully into the modern ecomonic era. It also announced that it will loosen government control of the media.

Despite continuing concerns, Qadhafi has come far in improving the image of Libya and of himself and in repairing relations with Western nations. Despite unpredictability, Qadhafi provides stability in the Arab world and an ally against Islamic fundamentalism. Libya remains on friendly terms with most Arab and African nations too. Libyan citizens and international leaders are beginning to wonder what will happen when Qadhafi—sixty-four years old in 2006—is no longer Libya's leader, as the government is founded on his powerful personality.

⊙ Government

Libya's official name is the Great Socialist People's Libyan Arab Jamahiriya. *Jamahiriya* is a word coined by Muammar Qadhafi that translates into "state of the masses." The government structure is based on ideas in Qadhafi's *Green Book*. This book combines Socialist and Islamic theories and rejects political parties.

Billboards

Sayings of Libya's leader, Muammar Qadhafi, from his *Green Book*, are printed on giant billboards throughout the country. They display the leader's sometimes baffling political philosophy. Some of the slogans are:

"No representation in place of the people. Representation is fraud."

"Allowing profits means allowing exploitation"

"Partners not wage-workers"

"A man cannot be free if he lives in property he does not own"

"No democracy without popular congresses and committees everywhere"

"Committees everywhere"

"Democracy means popular rule not popular expression"

"Unity is necessary for strength"

"Forming parties splits society"

"All Libyans are Qadhafi"

"The land is never the property of anyone"

"Arab unity"

"The Quran is the law of society"

"In need, freedom is latent"

Under the direction of Qadhafi, the nation adopted people's committees, or local councils, as the basic unit of government. Although Qadhafi holds no formal office and calls himself the Brotherly Leader and Guide of the Revolution, he rules with absolute power as a military dictator. He is aided by a small group of trusted advisers, including family members.

The unicameral (one-body) legislature—the government's lawmaking branch—is known as the General People's Congress. The congress was established in 1977 to replace the Revolutionary Command Council. All the congress's representatives—elected by local people's committees—are members of the Arab Socialist Union.

The General People's Congress members elect the General People's Committee, a cabinet, or group of advisers. The cabinet oversees major ministries (government agencies) including economic affairs, public health, housing, energy, and justice. Most of these ministries are located outside of the capital, in Benghazi, Al-Kufrah, and other cities. The prime minister, elected by the congress (Shukri Ghanim was elected in June 2003), is the head of the government.

More than six hundred local people's committees govern businesses, towns, trade unions, and other institutions, such as universities. People's committees also lead the twenty-five *baladiyat*, or provinces. Adults over the age of eighteen elect the members of these committees.

Libya's justice system is based on Italian civil law and traditional Islamic law. The Supreme Court in Tripoli decides important criminal and constitutional cases. Lower courts include courts of appeal in Benghazi, Tripoli, and Sabha. These chambers hear appeals from the country's lowest courts. These are located in almost all communities. Special courts, including military courts, try political offenses and crimes against the state.

 Visit www.vgsbooks.com to find links to more information about Muammar Qadhafi and the Libyan government.

THE PEOPLE

With the inhospitable Sahara covering most of Libya, the nation has always had a very low population density. The country averages 8 persons per square mile (3 per sq. km). In the interior, this figure falls to less than 1 person per square mile (less than 1 per sq. km). But about 90 percent of the 5.6 million Libyans live near the Mediterranean coast, where all of the cities and large towns have been built. The population density in this part of the country rises to 80 persons per square mile (31 per sq. km).

Libya's population growth rate is 2.4 percent. Some of this growth is due to large numbers of immigrants from other parts of Africa. These people come seeking work in the oil-rich country. Women in Libya have an average of 3.7 children each. Libya has a youthful population, with 35 percent of the Libyan population under the age of fifteen. With so many young people, the population is expected to keep growing. By the year 2050, it is estimated that Libya will have a population of 10.8 million people.

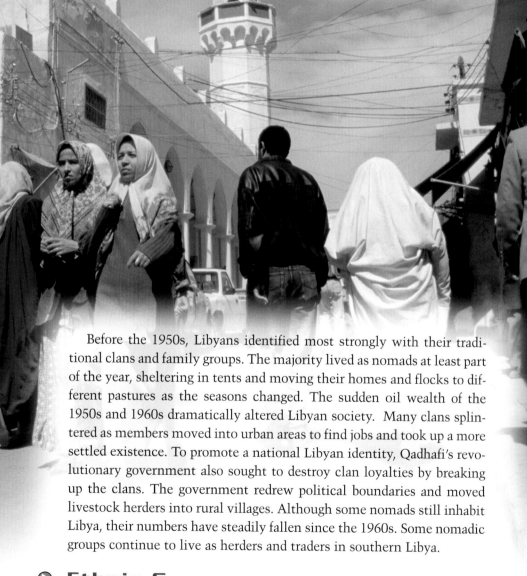

Before the 1950s, Libyans identified most strongly with their traditional clans and family groups. The majority lived as nomads at least part of the year, sheltering in tents and moving their homes and flocks to different pastures as the seasons changed. The sudden oil wealth of the 1950s and 1960s dramatically altered Libyan society. Many clans splintered as members moved into urban areas to find jobs and took up a more settled existence. To promote a national Libyan identity, Qadhafi's revolutionary government also sought to destroy clan loyalties by breaking up the clans. The government redrew political boundaries and moved livestock herders into rural villages. Although some nomads still inhabit Libya, their numbers have steadily fallen since the 1960s. Some nomadic groups continue to live as herders and traders in southern Libya.

Ethnic Groups

The large majority, about 97 percent, of Libyans are Arabs, who trace their ancestry to the intermarriage of Arab and Berber groups after the

A Berber man waits with his herd of camels. Descendants of desert nomads, present-day Berbers still maintain a lifestyle similar to their ancestors.

Arab invasions of the seventh century. Some Arabs are Bedouins, an Arabic subgroup, who chiefly live as nomads in the desert.

The rest of the population includes several small but distinct ethnic groups. Ethnic Berbers live mostly in the highland regions of northern and western Libya. They claim to be descendants of Libya's original inhabitants. In various towns west of Tripoli, Berber dialects are commonly heard, and Berber place-names have survived in the Nafusah Plateau. Imazighan, their ancient name, is sometimes still used to refer to Berbers. Their long-standing resistance to foreign rule gives them a reputation of independence of spirit. Most Berbers are Kharijite Muslims, a sect that resists the Arab monopoly on Islamic leadership. Many Berbers support themselves as farmers or as nomadic herders who live in tents with their extended families. Berber women are generally independent, managing their own finances and engaging in trade at markets.

The Tuareg peoples cross national borders. They inhabit southwestern Libya, as well as parts of nearby Algeria, Mali, and Niger. The total Tuareg population numbers about two million people, but only a fraction of them live in Libya. They trace their origins to a society of Berber nomads. Tuareg caravans carried on the trans-Saharan trade for centuries. Some modern Tuareg engage in trade between countries and still rely on camels as being more versatile in the desert than trucks. The Tuareg speak a Berber language, Tamacheq, and write in an ancient script known as *tifnagh*. The Tuareg follow Islam but have some religious and social customs of their own. For example, Tuareg men cover their faces with veils of dark blue, almost black. As a result, Tuareg are sometimes called People of the Black Veil, or the Blue Men. The women do not cover their faces, and Tuareg women and men have equal social status. Terrible droughts in the 1980s changed the Tuareg

A Tuareg man wearing the traditional dark blue veil pours a glass of tea, a traditional drink among many Libyans.

nomadic lifestyle as thousands of people and their herds of animals died. Many of these proud and independent people were forced to settle as farmers or to work as seasonal laborers.

The Tebu, who live in the Al-Kufrah Oasis and in the Tibesti Mountains straddling Libya and northern Chad, have been an important central Saharan group for centuries. Like the Tuareg, the Tebu historically were tough and solitary nomads. The Tebu are Muslims whose religious beliefs were strongly molded by the Sanusi Brotherhood. Divided into at least twenty large clans, the Tebu now number only about five thousand within Libya. They live in one of the most isolated regions of the Sahara and have remained largely free of outside control, highly valuing their independence.

 For links to more information about Libya's population, visit www.vgsbooks.com.

The Libyan population also includes a number of skilled and unskilled foreign workers who help Libya meet its labor needs. The exact number of foreign workers is not available, but estimates are many hundreds of thousands. Most are Africans, including North Africans from Egypt and Tunisia, as well as sub-Saharan Africans. Black Africans, mostly from sub-Saharan countries, have been the victims of growing resentment and racism against migrant workers. In 2000 antiblack violence erupted into riots and expulsions from the country of thousands of non-Arab Africans.

A truckload of **African migrant workers** come to Libya in search of work.

Italians, Indians, Pakistanis, and Turks also have jobs in the country's various industrial, communications, and natural resources projects. Tripoli has small neighborhoods of Greeks and Maltese, who work in the fishing industry. After the end of international sanctions in 2003 and 2004, the oil industry opened to European and U.S. companies again, expanding the need for workers.

Language

Arabic is the official language of Libya. A Semitic (southwestern Asian) tongue with origins on the Arabian Peninsula, Arabic spread to North Africa during the Arab invasions of the seventh century. Arabic exists in many forms and has various dialects, or regional variations. Classical Arabic—the language of the Quran—is an international tongue used mainly by religious scholars and teachers. Journalists, teachers, and scientists use literary Arabic. Within Libya, many local and regional dialects of Arabic are spoken. Many Libyans in the major cities understand English and Italian.

Some Berbers of northwestern Libya speak both Arabic and Numidian, an ancient African language. Villagers and nomads of the Nafusah Plateau and other regions with large Berber populations also use dialects of the Berber language. Berber is related to Ancient Egyptian but uses the Arabic script.

The Tuareg speak one of four main dialects of Tamacheq. Speakers of different dialects can mostly understand each other. The Tuareg sometimes call themselves Kel Tamacheq, which means "People of the Tamacheq Language." Ancient inscriptions of the tifnagh script have been found on rock surfaces in the Sahara.

Health and Housing

Libya provides free health care and medicines to its citizens, as well as public clinics and hospitals. The country's two largest hospitals are in

Tripoli and Benghazi, but even many small towns have well-equipped clinics. Medical colleges in Libya train doctors, dentists, and nurses, and many doctors have been educated overseas. Libya has 1.3 physicians and 4.3 hospital beds for every 1,000 people. Libya's infant mortality rate, an important measure of a nation's public health, stands at 28 deaths out of every 1,000 live births—a figure well below North Africa's average of 51 deaths out of 1,000 live births. Abortion is permitted only in cases where the mother's life is in danger.

Health conditions are generally good. Some illnesses, including malaria and the eye disease trachoma, have been brought under control. Other diseases, including typhoid, hepatitis, meningitis, and venereal diseases, remain a challenge to the health-care system. The rate of AIDS (acquired immunodeficiency syndrome) is a relatively low 0.2 percent. Immigration from sub-Sahara countries where AIDS is epidemic threatens to spread the deadly disease.

The public health system in Libya provides for health insurance, old-age pension, and payments to workers with job-related disabilities. Once dependent on their families for care, modern retirees have a social security system. Average life expectancy in Libya is 76 years, with men averaging 74 years and women averaging 78. The life expectancy for North Africa is 67 years.

Housing in cities, where most of the population lives, is similar to U.S. and European housing. About 97 percent of the population has access to sanitation. Downtown areas of large cities are full of modern apartment buildings with air-conditioning, electricity, and sewage

Laundry hangs from the balconies of an **apartment building in Sabha** while shoppers peruse vegetables at an outdoor market.

A village on the Nafusah Plateau shows traditional handmade building styles used in rural areas.

systems. However, immigration to the cities has caused overcrowding. In the countryside, people live in houses usually of handmade mud bricks covered with whitewash and topped with wooden roofs. Windows are small to keep out the sun. Nomadic people live in portable tents. In modern times, plastic sheeting is used to make tents, replacing the traditional cloth or leather tents.

◉ Education

Libya long suffered a serious lack of trained engineers and other professionals. Before World War II, few schools of any kind existed. At the time of independence, Libya's literacy rate, or rate of people able to read and write, was less than 10 percent.

Education improved greatly after the discovery of oil. Oil income was invested in schools and universities. After the 1969 revolution, more grade schools and secondary schools opened and the percentage of Libyan children—especially girls—attending school rapidly increased. In addition, more women began enrolling in the nation's universities and training schools. But an education gap remains between girls and boys, and the literacy rate reflects this gap. In the twenty-first century, only 68 percent of females are able to read and write compared to 91 percent of males.

Two schoolgirls from Sabha are on their way to class.

All levels of education, including college, are free of charge. Children are required to attend six years of coeducational (boys and girls together) primary school, starting at the age of six. They then attend six years of single-sex secondary school, which includes courses in English, science, and the humanities, and preparation either for college or trade school. Men who do not go to college must do two year's military service, and all men are supposed to serve one month in the military every year, though this is rarely enforced. Women must do one-time, four-month-long military training or industrial work.

Higher education in Libya is state-controlled. The country's first university was established in 1955 in Benghazi. By the mid-1990s, Tripoli and five other cities also had colleges. Al-Bayda is the site of a religious institute. Vocational schools in Libya offer training in commercial, industrial, and agricultural careers. There are also state-supported religious schools and training centers for teachers, and the Libyan government pays for some students to study abroad.

Family Life and Women

The family is of central importance to Libyan Arab society. Marriage is seen as the union of two families, not just two individuals. Young people are choosing their own marriage partners more and more, but marriages arranged by parents remain common. Weddings last for days, with hundreds of guests. Though only a small number practice

WOMEN IN THE GREEN BOOK

Qadhafi is famous for wanting to improve the status of women. He even has an all-female group of bodyguards. However, he also believes that motherhood is women's greatest and natural role and should be supported and protected.

Here are some of Qadhafi's ideas about women from his *Green Book*:

"There is no difference between man and woman in all that concerns humanity. None of them can marry the other against his or her will, or divorce without a just trial. Neither the woman nor the man can remarry without a previous agreement on divorce. The woman is the owner of the house because it is one of the suitable and necessary conditions for a woman who . . . cares for her children. The woman is the owner of the maternity shelter, which is the house. Even in the animal world, which differs in many ways from that of man, and where maternity is also a duty according to nature, it is coercion to deprive the young of their mother or deprive the female of her shelter."

Women in Libya enjoy more freedoms than women in stricter Arab Islamic countries.

it, polygamy (having more than one wife) is legal for men. However, a man must have the permission of the first wife before marrying a second.

The Arab family and society are patriarchal, or dominated by men. Men are the head of the households and leave the house to work or farm, while women traditionally stay home and take care of the children. People often live in extended family groups. Married men and their wives and children traditionally stay in the home of the man's parents, though many young couples are choosing to live on their own. Women's social life revolves around entertaining family, neighbors, and friends at home and visiting other homes. Men often socialize together in coffeehouses. Bars and nightclubs are illegal.

A Libyan family enjoys touring the Roman ruins at Leptis Magna.

Men and women pray separately in mosques. But Muslim women in Libya do not have to cover themselves with veils as they do in some conservative Islamic countries. The Quran instructs women—and men—to dress modestly, and this rule can be interpreted in different ways. Some women in Libya wear modern Western clothes, some wear a head scarf to cover their hair, and some cover themselves in a cloth that allows only one eye to be seen.

While traditional family roles remain strong, women's roles have changed since the late 1900s. The 1969 revolution gave women equal legal status with men. Marriage laws were changed so that a woman could not be married against her will or married younger than sixteen. Divorce laws were also made fairer. Women gained the right to own or sell property independently of male relatives. Government policies encouraged women to seek education and employment, and even encouraged women to go into traditionally male jobs, such as the police force. Equal pay for equal work was guaranteed. But many traditional attitudes remain, and women are only about 10 percent of the workforce. With more girls and women being educated, this percentage is increasing.

Bedouin, Berber, and Tuareg women do not experience the same social segregation as Arab women. They have long enjoyed greater freedoms and rights.

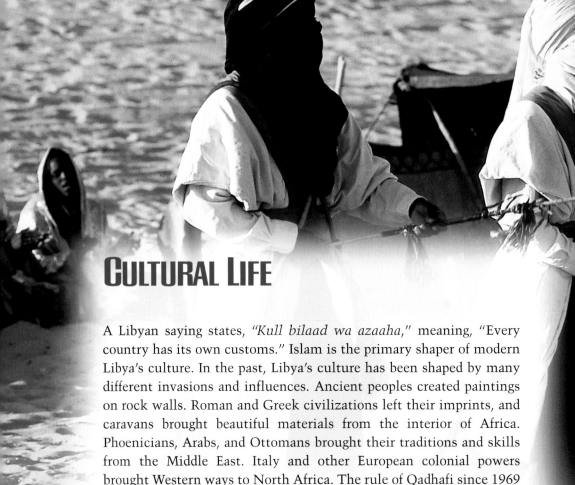

CULTURAL LIFE

A Libyan saying states, *"Kull bilaad wa azaaha,"* meaning, "Every country has its own customs." Islam is the primary shaper of modern Libya's culture. In the past, Libya's culture has been shaped by many different invasions and influences. Ancient peoples created paintings on rock walls. Roman and Greek civilizations left their imprints, and caravans brought beautiful materials from the interior of Africa. Phoenicians, Arabs, and Ottomans brought their traditions and skills from the Middle East. Italy and other European colonial powers brought Western ways to North Africa. The rule of Qadhafi since 1969 has imposed so much government control on individuals that an independent, modern Libyan culture has not yet fully evolved.

◉ Religion

About 97 percent of Libyans belong to the dominant Sunni sect of Islam. A small population of Libyans follow other branches of Islam, including Sufism, a mystical form of Islam. Sufis use music and dance

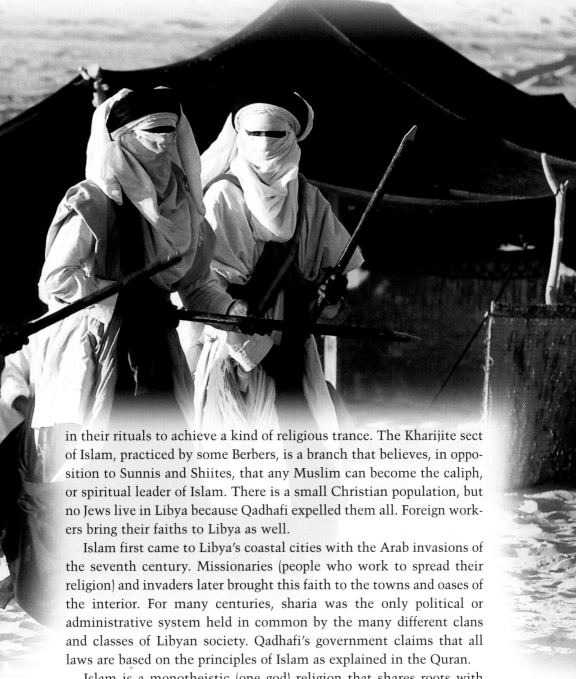

in their rituals to achieve a kind of religious trance. The Kharijite sect of Islam, practiced by some Berbers, is a branch that believes, in opposition to Sunnis and Shiites, that any Muslim can become the caliph, or spiritual leader of Islam. There is a small Christian population, but no Jews live in Libya because Qadhafi expelled them all. Foreign workers bring their faiths to Libya as well.

Islam first came to Libya's coastal cities with the Arab invasions of the seventh century. Missionaries (people who work to spread their religion) and invaders later brought this faith to the towns and oases of the interior. For many centuries, sharia was the only political or administrative system held in common by the many different clans and classes of Libyan society. Qadhafi's government claims that all laws are based on the principles of Islam as explained in the Quran.

Islam is a monotheistic (one god) religion that shares roots with Jewish and Christian religions. Muslims believe that the prophet Muhammad is the final messenger of God, completing the religious messages found in the Bible of Abraham, Moses, and Jesus, all of whom Muslims believe are prophets.

Devout Muslims observe the five pillars of Islam: making the statement of faith, "There is no god except Allah, and Muhammad is his prophet"; praying five times daily; fasting during the holy month of Ramadan; regular almsgiving (giving a percentage of one's income to charity); and making a pilgrimage to the holy city of Mecca, Saudi Arabia, if possible. Each Libyan village, town, and neighborhood has a mosque, from which a crier calls Muslims, five times daily, for prayer. Faithful Muslims stop what they are doing, wherever they are, to kneel, bow their foreheads to the ground, and pray.

In Libya, where Islam is the official state religion, the Islamic lunar calendar is observed for religious holidays. Months begin with each new

FROM PALM TREES TO MARBLE: THE DESIGN OF THE MOSQUE

The first Muslims gathered for prayer in the courtyard of the Prophet Muhammad's house. To create shade in the hot sun, they built an arcade, or arched, covered passageway, of branches propped up against palm trees at one end of the courtyard. Later mosques reflected this arrangement. A large courtyard leads to a hall supported by columns. Instead of palm trees, marble columns provide support. And painted, arched wooden ceilings take the place of branches. Inside the mosque, the mihrab (a recessed chamber, or niche, in a wall) indicates the direction of Mecca, where Muhammad was born. Muslims turn toward Mecca when they pray.

This mosque in Ghadamis, Libya, is built in the traditional style with arcades, minarets (towers), and domes.

moon, and the years are counted from Muhammad's journey from Mecca to Medina in 632. Libyans celebrate this journey, called the Hegira, each New Year's Day of the lunar calendar. Mouleed—held on the birth date of Muhammad—is a celebration of the life and faith of Muhammad. Ramadan is a holy month of prayer and fasting, believed to be the month when Allah called Muhammad to be his prophet. Muslims who observe Ramadan may not drink anything, smoke, or eat between sunrise and sunset. The end of Ramadan is announced with the sighting of the new moon and a feast.

Literature and Communications

Libya's twentieth-century literature and media was shaped by government control. The government controls the production and distribution of all printed matter, and few foreign books or magazines have been available. But in 2005, as part of the country's post-sanctions plans for modernization, the government announced that it would loosen its control of the media.

Libya's most popular book is the Quran, the Islamic holy book. Secular (nonreligious) literature is also written in Arabic, and Libya's literary themes have usually been political. Little has been translated into English. During the Italian colonial times, writers such as the poet Suleiman al-Baruni gave voice to people's resistance to foreign rule. After World War II, literature reflected themes of national independence and the challenges of living in a changing society. Hassan Saleh's *After the War* is an important book from this era. Literature after Qadhafi's takeover praised the achievements of the revolutionary regime and was strongly nationalistic. Some Libyans read *The Green Book*, a three-volume work by Muammar Qadhafi on the goals and ideals of his 1969 revolution. Ibrahim al-Kouni is Libya's

TRANSLITERATION

There is no standard system for transliterating, or converting, the Arabic alphabet into the Roman alphabet used to write English. Words are transliterated based on how they are pronounced, and pronunciation varies from region to region and person to person. It's as if everyone spelled English words based on how they heard them. Muammar Qadhafi's name, for instance, can be spelled dozens of different ways, including Gadaffi, Gheddafi, Qathafi, Kaddaffi, Kazzafi. . . . In addition, Arabic includes some sounds that are not represented in the Roman alphabet. For instance, the Arabic letter *ayn* represents a sound that has been described as sounding like someone being strangled.

Satellite dishes and a minaret punctuate the skyline of this Libyan desert town.

best-known modern writer. He is a full-time writer who lives in the desert part of the year. He writes essays, novels, and short stories. His famous short story, "The Drumming Sands," an ominous tale of death in the desert, has been translated into English.

Local Arabic newspapers and magazines are government controlled. Qadhafi started the newspaper the *Sun* before the revolution, and it is still in print. The *New Dawn* newspaper covers sports. A few foreign magazines, including *Time* and *Newsweek*, are available in Tripoli.

For links to online English-language newspapers from Libya, visit www.vgsbooks.com.

The radio is one of the most popular sources of communication in Libya. Several radio stations broadcast music, news, and religious programs. A national television network broadcasts mostly foreign programs with Arabic subtitles. People consider TV programs produced in Libya dreary as they largely feature hours of scenes of Qadhafi meeting dignitaries in his tent. Despite government control, however, satellite dishes for TV reception are legal. Most Libyans have them and are free to watch whatever they want.

Libya has a tiny film industry that makes mostly documentary films. Foreign films about Libya are also few. The story of the 1996 Academy Award-winning film, *The English Patient*, takes place in Libya but was filmed in the Sahara of neighboring Tunisia. *Lion of the Desert* was filmed in Libya in 1979 with Qadhafi's support. This generally accurate biography of Omar al-Mukhtar, the Libyan religious and guerrilla leader, features good footage of the eastern Libyan countryside.

Libyans have legal access to the Internet. There are 67 Internet hosts serving 160,000 Internet users. People can access the Internet at cybercafes in big cities. The national telecommunications system is being modernized, and there are 750,000 telephone lines in the country and 100,000 cellular phones.

Architecture and Art

Libyan architecture reflects the influence many different civilizations over the centuries. Ancient architecture in Libya can be seen in the superb Greek and Roman ruins of Sabratha, Leptis Magna, and Cyrene. The inhabitants of these cities left behind forums (public areas), theaters, baths, marketplaces, streets, shops, and homes. Archaeologists have also uncovered remains of the Garamantes civilization at the desert town of Germa. Early Berbers left behind fortified strongholds made of local stone. They were used to store valuables, including grain, and as protection in times of threat. Berbers also built underground houses as deep as three stories down. Caravan towns, such as Ghadamis and Ghat, display traditional building methods, utilizing mud brick and wood from palm trees. The mosques of Karamanli and Gurgi in Tripoli are among the best examples of Islamic architecture in the country. They have thin, narrow minarets and onion-shaped domes typical of Ottoman architecture. Inside, they are richly decorated with tile mosaics (pictures and designs

Mud brick walls in **Ghadamis** are covered with whitewash to reflect the sun's light and heat.

Hand-painted pottery, adorned with traditional geometric patterns and line work, reflects a style of Libyan artwork.

formed from tiny pieces of tile) and woodwork. Elegant, white Italian colonial architecture remains in use in Tripoli. Modern urban architecture, such as office and apartment buildings, tends to be undistinguished and utilitarian (useful rather than beautiful).

Libyan homes traditionally include handwoven wall and floor carpets as the main decoration. Muslims in Libya often carry a little prayer rug, used to kneel on for daily prayers wherever they are. Although small carpet factories still operate in Misratah and other cities, state ownership of the industry has caused a decline in production.

Berber and Arabic traditions dominate Libyan art. The art of the Berbers—as seen in carpets, embroidery, and jewelry—emphasizes complex shapes and lines. Berber women make distinctive carpets of sheep or goat's wool and are also famous for their decorated pottery. Some Berber women have facial tattoos of geometric designs signifying group affiliation. Forbidden by Islam from representing human forms in their works, artists in Libya mainly feature intricate lines and geometric patterns and designs in carpets, metalwork, leather goods, painted wall tiles, and pottery. Modern painters, such as Afaf al-Somali, a woman who specializes in watercolors, often paint landscapes. Libyan women decorate their hands for special occasions with intricate patterns drawn in red dye made from the desert henna plant. Calligraphy, or ornamental writing, turns the graceful Arabic script into a work of art found in Qurans and on tile work.

Music and Dance

Traditional folk songs and dances are popular throughout Libya. Traditional instruments include wood flutes, drums, lutes, and bagpipelike instruments. Folk dances reflect the patterns of daily life, reenacting, for instance, the motions of farming and harvesting. Music and dance are an important part of Libyan weddings. Libyan Arab men and women dance separately at these festive celebrations. In the cities, music and dance troupes perform regularly at festivals, in ceremonies, and on television. Tuareg musicians are mostly women. In one Tuareg dance, performed at New Year's festivities, women play drums while men on their best camels circle the women.

Modern music in Libya is dominated by the Egyptian pop music industry. But Mohammed Hassan is a well-known, popular Libyan singer. North African popular music often blends traditional Arab music with modern Western styles.

Holidays and Festivals

The Islamic month of Ramadan is the main religious holiday. Libyans also have a full calendar of national nonreligious holidays, using the Gregorian calendar that most Western countries use. Businesses close on these public holidays. March 2 is the Declaration of the People's Authority Day, with speeches and rallies marking the founding of the Jamahiriya. There are two Evacuation Day celebrations. The first is on March 28, when the British left Libya. The second takes place on June 11. Marking the evacuation of the Wheelus Air Force Base by the United States in 1970, this day is considered by Libyans to be the final defeat of the colonial powers in North Africa. On the country's biggest holiday, September 1, Revolution Day, the country celebrates Qadhafi's 1969 revolution with elaborate parades, fireworks, and speeches delivered by Qadhafi. A Day of Mourning is held on October 26, commemorating Libyans who died or went into exile during Italian rule. Everything, even telephone service, stops on this day. Libya celebrates its 1951 independence from Italy on December 24, Independence Day.

Local annual festivals in Ghadamis, Germa, Ghat, and other towns celebrate local culture in the unique style of each place. The oasis city of Houn, for instance, celebrates the arrival of spring with a candy-making festival.

Sports and Recreation

Young people throughout Libya play soccer in the open spaces of cities, villages, and oases. A popular team sport, soccer unites many Libyans in a shared enthusiasm, especially when the national team battles with its Middle Eastern and North African opponents. Many

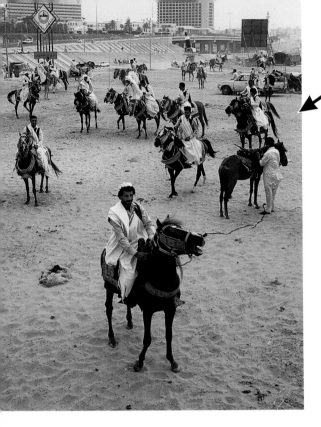

Libyan men prepare for a horse race on the outskirts of Tripoli. Libyans have long been proud of their Arabian horses, a breed noted for intelligence, spirit, and stamina.

Libyans also like to watch the ancient sport of horse racing. Racetracks in rural areas host contests among the fastest Arabian horses, as well as among the *maharis*, or racing camels. In the cities, athletes take part in basketball, track, and boxing events. Libyans also like to play chess and backgammon. Men gather to play these board games in coffee or tea shops. Women mostly socialize at home.

The first Libyan Olympic athletes participated in the Mexico City Olympic Games in 1968. But a terrorist incident during the 1972 games, partially blamed on Libya's government, led to the banning of Libya from Olympic contests until 1982. In 2004 eight athletes, including two women, participated in the Athens Olympic Games. They competed but won no medals in weight lifting, track and field, swimming, and tae kwon do.

Food

Libyan food has much in common with the cuisines of other North African nations. Couscous, one of the most popular dishes, is also well known in Tunisia, Algeria, and Morocco. To make couscous, cooks steam semolina (a wheat product) and serve it on a large platter with seasoned vegetables and meat. Steamed semolina also appears at breakfast mixed with honey and milk.

Libyans eat their largest meal at midday, before the day grows too hot. The most common meat is lamb. It is often cooked on a spit over an open fire. Following religious law, Muslims do not eat pork. Kabob is a mixture of chunks of lamb and other meat prepared on thin skewers. *Tajine*, a meat stew, may include mutton, lamb, beef, or chicken. *Shashokva*, roasted lamb in a tomato-based sauce, and *mouloqiyah* (steamed vegetables) are also popular. Most Libyan dishes also include a generous helping of peppers and spices.

Accompanying most Libyan meals is *kesrah*, a flat round bread. *Babaganoug*—a mixture of eggplant, olive oil, and sesame paste served with kesrah—may appear at the table at any time of the day. The evening meal is a lighter fare of fruits—dates, grapes, oranges, or other citrus fruits—and cheese. Libyans also enjoy yogurt made from goat's milk.

Thick black coffee is served throughout the day, as is sweet mint tea. Libyans drink fruit juices and bitter, a carbonated drink. According to Islamic tradition and Libyan law, alcoholic beverages are strictly banned.

SPICY BAKED FISH

Libyans like some of their dishes spicy hot. The original version of this Libyan recipe calls for twelve large jalapeño peppers. Because many Americans are not used to such hot food, this recipe suggests two peppers. If you like it hot, you can add more!

2 jalapeño peppers

juice of $1/2$ lemon

1 teaspoon ground cumin

$1/2$ teaspoon chili pepper

$1/2$ teaspoon salt

$1/2$ bunch cilantro, finely chopped

1 lb. white fish, such as cod or tilapia

2 tablespoons olive oil

1 small onion, chopped

2 cloves garlic, minced

2 tomatoes, chopped

1 cup tomato juice

1. Remove the seeds from the jalapeños, and chop the peppers into small pieces. (Be careful, jalapeño juice can burn—don't get any in your eyes.)
2. In a glass bowl, mix lemon juice, cumin, chili pepper, salt, and half of the cilantro. Add fish, making sure spice mix is spread over fish, and set aside.
3. In a large frying pan, heat olive oil over medium heat. Add jalapeños and onion and fry 10 minutes, stirring often.
4. Add fish with spices and garlic to pan. Fry fish 3 minutes on each side.
5. Add tomatoes and tomato juice. Heat until simmering (lightly boiling).
6. Carefully transfer all ingredients to glass baking dish. Cover dish and bake in 350°F oven for 20 minutes.
7. Serve hot, with the rest of the cilantro sprinkled on top. Serve with couscous, rice, or flat bread.

Serves 4

THE ECONOMY

Libya, an oil-rich country, has immense potential for economic growth. In the late twentieth century, large amounts of money were wasted through government inefficiency and corruption, military expenses, and costly attempts to develop weapons. Qadhafi also made large donations to developing countries in attempts to increase Libya's influence in Africa and elsewhere. International economic sanctions slowed the Libyan economy for years. The government's total control and mismanagement of the economy led to high inflation (general rise in prices), increased import prices, and an unemployment rate of 30 percent, resulting in a decline in the standard of living.

In the twenty-first century, Libya is transitioning from a Socialist economy—tightly controlled by the government—to a more open, market-based economy. After the final lifting of international economic sanctions in 2004, the government announced ambitious plans to increase foreign investment in the oil and gas sectors and to raise production significantly. This promises jobs for the unemployed. The government is also

pursuing development projects such as building and improving highways, railways, telecommunications systems, and irrigation. Continued investment in education will guarantee a skilled workforce in the future.

In 2005 Libya announced an economic reform plan, laying the groundwork to bring the country fully into the modern economic era. The plan hopes to make the government more efficient, speed up privatization (the private ownership of business), and create a more open media. Libya's industries and agriculture are growing along with its population, and the country has huge reserves of oil and natural gas to draw on for export income. However, Libya's dependence on a single, nonrenewable resource causes uncertainty for the country's long-term future.

Oil and Other Mining

Earnings from oil make up 25 percent of Libya's gross domestic product (GDP, the value of the goods and services produced each year in a country). The oil industry employs 10 percent of the country's workforce. Oil contributes practically all—more than 95 percent—of Libya's earnings from exports, bringing billions of dollars a year into the country.

Libya has the largest reserves of oil in Africa and the eleventh-largest in the world. Libya's high-grade oil is in high demand. It is low in sulfur, making it ideal for gasoline production, easy to refine, and less polluting. The country's location near Europe is also an advantage, allowing Libya to transport oil more cheaply than can other oil-producing nations in the Middle East and Africa. Western Europe mostly did not join the United States in their boycott of Libyan oil.

In 2005 U.S. oil companies returned to Libya after more than a twenty-year absence. They joined other foreign oil companies eager to pay hundreds of millions of dollars for rights to explore new areas for oil. After winning a contract, each company spends many more millions on oil exploration in this underexplored country. If the companies find oil or gas, they receive a certain percentage of production. Libya's state-owned oil company receives the rest and refines and markets the fuel on its own. Pipelines carry crude oil to refineries at oil terminals on the Mediterranean coast. Tankers carry the refined petroleum to Europe's enormous energy market. The relatively quick travel time to the United States—about half the time it takes Saudi Arabian crude oil—adds to the attraction for U.S. oil companies as well.

Natural gas, a by-product of oil drilling, is also an important energy export. Although engineers estimate that Libya only has enough oil in its existing known deposits to last until about 2070, the country has huge natural gas reserves that could last for several more centuries.

Libya has few mineral resources besides oil. Iron ore from a large strip mine near Sabha supplies raw material to an iron and steel plant at Misratah. Workers draw salt from marshes and depressions near the coast, and small deposits of limestone, gypsum, and marble provide building materials.

 Visit www.vgsbooks.com to find links to more information about Libya's oil industry.

● Industry and Trade

The non-oil industrial sector provides Libya with 20 percent of its GDP. Industry employs 19 percent of the workforce.

Libya has successfully built up a manufacturing sector, but these businesses are still closely tied to and dependent on the oil industry. The construction industry, for instance, serves the needs of the oil industry by building refineries, buildings, roads, and other structures. Other industry includes the production of petrochemicals, iron, steel, and aluminum. Factories also make steel pipes, drums, and other equipment for the oil-drilling industry. When oil income declines because of falling prices, less money is available to import the raw materials needed for factories.

Libya has expanded its non-oil manufacturing and construction sectors. The most important nonpetroleum manufactured goods are food products—such as olive oil, beverages, dates, and citrus fruit—textiles, handicrafts, and cement for the large construction trade. The textile industry makes clothing, leather goods, and shoes. Small handicraft industries employ carpet weavers, metalsmiths, and leather workers.

Since the 1960s, the export of oil has been Libya's principal product of foreign trade. Libya also exports animal hides and food. Oil has provided the country with a large trade surplus, meaning the country earns more from the sale of its exports than it spends on imports. Libya has a reserve of $20 billion. The most important buyers of Libyan exports are Italy, Spain, Germany, and Turkey. Libya purchases machinery,

Women piece together cloth at a **textile factory** in Tripoli.

A craftsman weaves a carpet on a loom. Many Libyans earn a living by making and selling handmade goods.

cars, basic manufactured goods, transportation equipment, consumer goods, and food mainly from Italy, Germany, Tunisia, Great Britain, and France.

Foreign investment is important to the Libyan economy. European nations, including Britain and Italy, built the country's first manufacturing enterprises, and foreign oil companies continue to develop Libya's oil drilling, shipping, and refining facilities.

Agriculture and Fishing

Agriculture provides 9 percent of Libya's GDP. Agricultural workers make up 17 percent of the workforce. Once largely agricultural, Libya does not have enough fertile land to feed its largely urban population. Hot, dry conditions and poor soils severely limit agriculture, while higher incomes and a growing population have caused food consumption to rise. Domestic food production meets only about 25 percent of demand, and Libya relies on foreign imports for three-quarters of its food needs.

About 1 percent of the land is under cultivation, and 8 percent is used for pasture. Farms are usually small, averaging 27 acres (11 hectares) and farmed by the families that own them. Large farms utilize machinery, but the average family farm relies on traditional, non-mechanized tools. To better meet the country's food needs, the government is building the Great Man Made River to bring water from underground aquifers in the Sahara to dry tracts near the coast.

The most important agricultural regions in Libya are the Al-Jifarah Plain near Tripoli and the Al-Marj Plain near Benghazi. Wheat and barley are the principal cereal crops, while millet is planted in Fezzan. Olive groves cover parts of the Al-Jifarah Plain and the Nafusah Plateau, producing olives and olive oil. Libyan farmers also harvest almonds,

Two men stand on one of the huge pipelines designated for use in the **Great Man Made River project.** The project, which is scheduled to be completed in 2034, will provide the country with much-needed water pumped from below the desert's surface. So far, about 5 million tons (4.5 million metric tons) of cement have been used to make the pipes for the Great Man Made River project.

dates, citrus fruits, onions, potatoes, peanuts, soybeans, and tobacco.

Sheep, goats, cattle, camels, and poultry are the main livestock. Raising livestock traditionally has been an economically important agricultural activity in Libya. Sheep, which make up the largest and most productive herds, supply meat, milk, and wool.

Fish are plentiful in the waters off Libya's coast. A small fishing fleet operates out of the port of Tripoli and along the country's northwestern coast. Italians, Greeks, and Maltese do most of the fishing. Fishing boats haul in tuna, sardines, and mullet for a small domestic market. Libya has granted Greek fishing companies control of underwater sponge harvesting. Libya is encouraging foreign investment in the fishing sector.

◑ Services and Tourism

The service sector is made up of economic activities that provide services rather than goods. This sector includes jobs in government, banking, retail trade, education, health care, and tourism. The service sector in Libya accounts for 46 percent of the GDP and employs 54 percent of the working population.

Libya is opening up to business and tourism in the twenty-first century. When the UN first suspended some of its sanctions in 1999, visitors to Libya jumped to 963,000, earning the country $28 million. As Libya reconnects with the rest of the world, tourism offers the largest opportunities for growth. The country has much to offer: monuments, cities, and gorgeous landscapes. With more than 1,000 miles (1,609 km) of undeveloped Mediterranean coastline, Libya is planning holiday spots for tourists looking for sun, sand, and sea. Five UNESCO (a UN agency) World Heritage sites are located in the country: Leptis Magna, Sabratha, Cyrene, Ghadamis, and prehistoric rock art sites at Tadrart Acacus. The country is investing in this opportunity. Plans are under way to build hotels, improve transportation, and develop sites to handle visitors.

Transportation

Libyans have about 53,000 miles (84,000 km) of roads, with about 31,000 miles (50,000 km) of them paved. The busiest route is a coastal highway that skirts the shores of the Mediterranean Sea from Tunisia to Egypt. Other highways extend from this route southward to the oases of Sabha and Al-Kufrah. Public buses run between cities and towns, providing the most important means of transportation in Libya. Only one in seven Libyans owns an automobile. Although cars and trucks can survive desert travel, many desert dwellers depend on the hardy camel to cross the hot and waterless Saharan spaces. Although Libya has no finished railways, the government is planning a railway system.

Libya's largest and busiest port is Tripoli. It accommodates cargo ships as well as passenger ferries that sail to the Mediterranean island of Malta. Both Tripoli and Benghazi handle commercial shipments of heavy equipment and raw materials. Mersa Brega, a terminal point for several large pipelines, is the biggest of the ports used for the shipment of refined oil.

Libya has four large commercial airports—at Tripoli, Benghazi, Sabha, and Misratah. The state operates Jamahiriya Libyan Arab Airlines as the national carrier.

The Future

Libya is poised in a position of great possibility. The country's oil wealth is its greatest economic asset. Other countries are eager to be on friendly terms with a government that offers them oil business.

Qadhafi has come far in repairing his image as a supporter of world terrorism. Once a threat to world peace, Libya has given up its weapons programs. An Arab Islamic country, Libya does not support radical fundamentalism but offers a stable government in

---

FATHER AND SON LOOK TO THE FUTURE

Muammar Qadhafi outlined his new vision of an internationally friendly Libya in September 2000: "Now is the era of economy, consumption, markets, and investments. This is what unites people irrespective of language, religion, and nationalities."

Saif al-Islam Qadhafi, son of Muammar, attended the 2005 World Economic Forum in Switzerland. "The old times are finished and Libya is ready to move onto the new stage of modernization," Saif al-Islam said in an interview. "But of course success can only be measured by the implementation."

A young clerk sells Western-style clothing at an upscale men's clothing store in Tripoli. A young, educated population is Libya's best hope for the future.

an unstable part of the world. Qadhafi's son, Saif, is viewed by the West as a stabilizing political influence.

Under Qadhafi, the country has developed good education, health care, and social service systems. Libya still imports 75 percent of its food but can afford to do so. The Great Man Made River and desalination plants meet the country's freshwater needs. The infrastructure, such as roads and communications systems, continues to develop. Investments in tourism are a good bet to take advantage of the dramatic beauty and history Libya has to offer.

But the future remains uncertain. Oil is a nonrenewable resource that will not last forever, and Libya depends on it for most of its income and energy. Water under the Sahara is being drained by the GMR, and desert peoples are already suffering from drought. Libya is part of the Arab world, which struggles with internal terrorism and international conflicts. Qadhafi has turned to the African continent to build alliances, but that continent has many areas of strife, poverty, and unstable governments. Qadhafi has been an unpredictable leader in world politics in the past, and he continues to rule his country as a dictator. As Qadhafi works with other countries and Libya opens to the world again, the possibility of meeting these challenges successfully becomes more of a reality.

8000 B.C.	Farmers and nomads live in Libya.
CA. 3000 B.C.	The Imazighan (Berbers) arrive from southwestern Asia and gradually spread across North Africa. Climate changes are creating the Sahara.
CA. 1300 B.C.	Phoenicians from modern Lebanon begin building settlements along the coast of North Africa for trade.
631 B.C.	Greek settlers establish Euhesperides (modern Benghazi), one of their colonies in a region known as Cyrenaica, named for the Greek settlement of Cyrene.
46 B.C.	The Roman emperor Julius Caesar establishes the Roman province of Africa Nova (New Africa), including Libyan lands. Camels, introduced around this time, increase the trans-Saharan caravan trade.
A.D. 395	Conflict within the Roman Empire divides the empire. In Libya most Romans have adopted Christianity.
431	The Vandals conquer Roman Libya and destroy much of Roman culture there.
644	Arab Muslim forces have gained control of Libya.
1000s	Arab clans known as the Bedouin invade North Africa.
1510	Spain attacks and loots Tripoli. Piracy on the Barbary Coast flourishes.
1551	Tripoli and the surrounding area become an Ottoman province.
1711	Ahmed Karamanli founds an independent dynasty within the Ottoman Empire.
1801	The United States blockades Tripoli, and Libyans seize the USS *Philadelphia*.
1830s	Islamic scholar and holy man Sidi Muhammad Ali al-Sanusi (known as the Grand Sanusi) establishes the Sanusi Brotherhood in Libya.
1911	Italian forces capture Tripoli and bring most of Libya under Italian colonial rule.
1914	Libya fights on the losing side against Italy in World War I.
1922	Al-Aziziyah, Libya, reaches 136°F (58°C), the highest temperature ever recorded on earth.
1931	The Italian colonial government executes guerrilla leader Omar al-Mukhtar.
1942	British forces defeat the Germans in North Africa during World War II and occupy Libya.

1951 Libya gains independence with King Idris as its leader, and Tripoli becomes its capital. The literacy rate among Libyans is less than 10 percent.

1955 Libya's first university is founded in Benghazi.

1959 The beginning of economic prosperity for Libya occurs when engineers discover large reserves of oil under the desert there.

1960s Devastating droughts kill thousands of Tuareg people and their herds of animals, and many Tuareg are forced to end their nomadic way of life.

1969 Colonel Muammar Qadhafi and his supporters seize control of Libya, overthrow King Idris's government, and abolish the monarchy. Women begin to gain equal legal status with men.

1973 A cultural revolution to transform Libya into a purely Arab, Socialist state begins. Libyan forces occupy Aozou Strip in northern Chad.

1984 The Libyan government begins the Great Man Made River (GMR) project to bring water from under the desert to dry but fertile areas in the north.

1988 Libyan agents place a bomb on Pan Am jetliner 103, which explodes over Lockerbie, Scotland. The United Nations places international sanctions on Libya.

1994 Libya returns the Aozou Strip to Chad.

1999 Qadhafi surrenders the Libyans suspected of the Pan Am bombing for trial.

2003 UN sanctions on Libya are lifted. Libya announces it will end its programs to develop weapons of mass destruction as well as chemical and biological weapons.

2004 The United States ends its economic sanctions against Libya.

2005 The Libyan government announces plans to bring the country fully into the modern economic era. It also announces that it will loosen government control of the media. U.S. oil companies return to Libya.

COUNTRY NAME Great Socialist People's Libyan Arab Jamahiriya (Libya)

AREA 679,358 square miles (1,759,537 sq. km)

MAIN LANDFORMS Mediterranean Region, Sahara, Libyan Desert, Sirte Desert, Awbari Sand Sea, Murzuq Sand Sea, Al-Jifarah Plain, Al-Marj Plain, Nafusah Plateau, Al-Akhdar Mountains (Green Mountains), Tibesti Mountains

HIGHEST POINT Bikku Bitti, 7,436 feet (2,266 m) above sea level

LOWEST POINT Sabkhat Ghuzayyil, 154 feet (47 m) below sea level

MAJOR RIVERS none

ANIMALS addaxes, butterflies, camels, eagles, falcons, fennecs, gulls, gazelles, hyenas, jackals, jerboas, lizards, locusts, scorpions, snakes, spiders, terns, vultures, wildcats

CAPITAL CITY Tripoli

OTHER MAJOR CITIES Benghazi, Misratah, Tobruk, Sabha

OFFICIAL LANGUAGE Arabic

MONETARY UNITY Libyan dinar (LYD) 1,000 dirhams = 1 dinar

LIBYAN CURRENCY

Libyan coins come in denominations of 1, 5, 10, 20, and 100 dirhams. Bills, or paper money, are in amounts of $^1/_4$, $^1/_2$, 1, 5, 10, and 20 dinars. Coins carry the Libyan coat of arms, a hawk with a banner in its feet. On the banner is the country's name. Bills have illustrations on them. The 1-dinar bill, for instance, carries a picture of Qadhafi on one side and a mosque on the other. Camels are seen on the 5-dinar bill, and Omar al-Mukhtar is on the 10-dinar bill.

In September 1969, after the Libyan revolution, Libya adopted its own flag. When Libya joined the Union of the Arab Republics in 1970, their flag became the official Libyan flag. In March 8, 1977, Libya's official name was changed to Al-Jamahiriya Al-Arabiya Al-Libiyah Ash-Shabiya Al-Ishtrakia Al-Uzma (Great Socialist People's Libyan Arab Jamahiriya). On November 11, 1977, Libya adopted its own flag, the current flag. It is entirely green with no symbols at all. Green is the color of Islam, and the flag reflects Qadhafi's commitment to the religion.

"Allahu Akbar Fawqa Kayd Al-Motadi"
(God Is Greater Than the Aggressor's Malice!)

"Allahu Akbar," the first words of the song of the anthem of this Islamic North African state, are also the first words of the Muslim call to prayer. Originally, the song was written as a battle song of the Egyptian army during the Suez War against Israel in 1956. When Muammar Qadhafi took over control of Libya in 1969, he adopted this song as the Libyan national anthem. The words in Arabic are by Mahmoud El-Sherif and the music is by Abdalla Shams El-Din.

God is greatest!
God is greatest!
He is above plots of the aggressors,
And He is the best helper of the oppressed.
With faith and with weapons I shall defend my country,
And the light of truth will shine in my hand.
Sing with me!
Sing with me!
God is greatest!
God is greatest!
God, God, God is greatest!
God is above the aggressors.

 For a link to a site where you can listen to Libya's national anthem, visit www.vgsbooks.com.

MOHAMMED HASSAN (b. 19??) Hassan, Libya's best-known singer, is a native of Al-Khums. His music is in traditional Arab style, but his subject matter is Libyan, and includes songs of praise for Qadhafi. He also sings love songs.

KHADIJAH AL-JAHMI (1921–1996) Born in Benghazi, al-Jahmi is considered a role model for modern Libyan women. Her father was committed to her education, and her teacher was a leading Libyan woman, Hameedah al-Anaizi. At a very young age, al-Jahmi memorized the Quran. She later studied in Egypt, then returned to Libya, where she taught for several years before joining the Libyan Broadcasting Company. Al-Jahmi became the first Libyan anchorwoman. She hosted a radio show called *Rukn al-Marah* (Woman's Corner) and was respected as a professional. In 1966 al-Jahmi started a magazine called *al-Marah* (The Woman), which dealt with women's issues. In the 1970s, she created *al-Amal* (The Hope) magazine to deal with children's issues. She also founded an organization for preschool children and a children's summer camp. In retirement, she continued to write for young Libyan women. Al-Jahmi is remembered as a pioneer, a role model, and a generous teacher.

IBRAHIM AL-KOUNI (b. 1948) Born in Ghadamis, al-Kouni is Libya's best-known modern writer, known throughout the Arab world. He studied in Moscow, Russia, and lived in Warsaw, Poland, where he was in charge of the Libyan People's Bureau. He returned to Libya and lives in the desert for part of each year. Some of his work, including his famous tale of death in the desert, "The Drumming Sands," has been translated into English. He publishes short stories, novels, and essays.

NASSER MIZDAWI (b. 1950) Born in Tripoli, Mizdawi was a pioneer of a new form of pop music that emerged in North Africa in the early 1970s. This new music was a fusion of local Arabic music with European pop, as well as African influences. This music especially influenced young, urban Arab performers. Mizdawi has performed internationally and released his latest album in 2000.

OMAR AL-MUKHTAR (1858–1931) Nicknamed the Lion of the Desert, Omar was a hero of the Libyan resistance against Italian military rule. He also was a religious figure, the leader of a small Sanusi community with simple, quiet, and scholarly personal habits. In 1923, however, in response to the increase in Italy's violent conquest of Libya, he organized desert peoples into bands of resisters and arranged for military supplies to be smuggled to them so they could fight against modern machine guns and armored cars. He personally commanded his own band of up to five hundred fighters, which formed the core of the resistance movement. The Italians intensified their harsh treatment and, after years of fighting, captured the seventy-three-year-old Omar and executed him.

MUAMMAR QADHAFI (b. 1942) Qadhafi was born in a tent in the Sirte Desert, near Surt. His parents were Bedouin people, and he was the first member of his family to learn to read and write. While still in high school, Qadhafi became politically active on behalf of Arab unity. His devotion to this cause was inspired by his nationalist heroes, Omar al-Mukhtar and Egyptian president Gamal Nasser. In 1965 Qadhafi graduated from a military academy in Benghazi and went for more army training to England. In 1969 he led a military coup that toppled King Idris and ended the monarchy. Qadhafi assumed leadership of Libya and has remained the dictator of the country. Considered eccentric and unpredictable, Qadhafi has changed his positions on many political questions but remains firm in his support of Arab and African unity. He is a devout Muslim, praying regularly and not drinking alcohol, but he is progressive in his belief in female equality. He is married, after one divorce, and has eight children. His only living daughter is a lawyer.

SAIF AL-ISLAM QADHAFI (b. 1972) The son of Muammar Qadhafi, Saif graduated from the London School of Economics. He is the head of an official charity, the Gaddafi International Foundation for Charity Associations, which has intervened in various hostage situations involving Islamic militants. He is widely thought of as Qadhafi's heir, though he himself points out that there is no hereditary leadership in the nation. Saif has spoken out for democracy and is popular among many young Libyans.

SIDI MUHAMMAD IDRIS AL-SANUSI [KING IDRIS I] (1890–1983) Idris was the last king of Libya, ruling from 1951 to 1969. His grandfather was the founder of the Sanusi Brotherhood. He inherited his grandfather's position and became the emir of Cyrenaica. In 1922 Idris went to Egypt, which served as his base in a guerrilla war against Italian colonial rule. During World War II, Idris supported the Allies against Germany, which occupied Libya. With the defeat of the Germans, he united Libya and was proclaimed king of Libya upon independence in 1951. To the displeasure of Arab nationalists, Idris maintained close ties with the West. While Idris was in Turkey for medical treatment, he was overthrown by Muammar Qadhafi. Idris lived in exile in Cairo, Egypt, until his death.

SEPTIMIUS SEVERUS (145–211) Septimius was born in Leptis Magna to a wealthy, influential family. The first North African to become emperor, he ruled the Roman Empire from 193 to 211. His reign saw advances in the Roman legal system, which would influence law until the present day. With his wife, Julia Domna, he also sponsored philosophical, religious, and military excellence. He encouraged architecture and the improvement of towns, both in Rome and in Leptis Magna and others cities in Roman North Africa.

While Libya has some of the world's best classical sites, stunning landscapes, and is newly welcoming tourists, the U.S. Department of State has issued a 2005 travel warning: "Although Libya appears to have curtailed its support for international terrorism, it may maintain residual contacts with some of its former terrorist clients. Recent worldwide terrorist alerts have stated that extremist groups continue to plan terrorist attacks against U.S. interests in the region." Check the State Department's website at http://www.state.gov/travel/ for updates.

BENGHAZI Excavations in this ancient city have uncovered ruins from the 500s B.C. In modern Benghazi, Arab architecture combines with modern skyscrapers and traditional open-air markets are found next to modern supermarkets.

CYRENE This city was founded in the seventh century B.C. The city's Sanctuary of Zeus, the biggest Greek temple in Africa, was built in the sixth century B.C. The beautiful Greek and Roman ruins make up one of the most complex archaeological sites in the Mediterranean region.

GHADAMIS Settled by the Romans in 19 B.C., this oasis settlement was located on the first part of the Saharan caravan route. Visitors can see excellent examples of Berber desert architecture here.

LEPTIS MAGNA This is one of the best-preserved classical sites in the world. Magnificent ruins of public monuments, baths, marketplaces, theaters, villas, and residential areas can be seen in what was one of the most beautiful cities of the Roman Empire. An extensive and well-designed museum helps visitors explore and understand the ancient city.

SABRATHA Originally a Phoenician port city, Sabratha was rebuilt by the Romans in the A.D. 200s. Visitors can tour the large excavation that uncovered a forum area (open gathering space), impressive theater, temples, and arch of victory. There is also a museum on the site.

TADRART ACACUS This city is on Libya's southwest border, near the city of Ghat. It makes a good base for visitors who want to view the thousands of rock art sites in the area, dating from 8000 B.C. to A.D. 100. The changing plants, animals, and human cultures of this Saharan region are recorded in the cave paintings of different styles.

TRIPOLI Roman ruins and old mosques mingle with modern buildings in this coastal city that is the center of modern Libya. The history of continuous settlement can be seen in the superb collection of the archaeological museum.

Arabic: the official language of Libya. Classical Arabic is the language of the Quran.

caliph: a spiritual leader of Islam, a successor of the Prophet Muhammad

couscous: a coarse-ground grain, such as semolina, which is steamed and served with many dishes

desertification: fertile land turning into barren land. It is caused by change of climate, drought, or overuse of dry lands.

GDP: gross domestic product, the value of domestic goods and services produced in a country over a period of time, usually a year

henna: a dye made from plants and used to color hair or paint designs on skin

Islam: a religion founded in the seventh century A.D. based on the teachings of the Prophet Muhammad. Islam has two major sects, Shiite and Sunni. The holy book of Islam is the Quran.

jamahiriya: an Arabic word coined by Qadhafi meaning "state of the masses"

medina: Arabic for "town" or "city"; used to refer to a city's old central section

mosque: an Islamic place of worship and prayer

Muslim: a follower of Islam

nationalist: a person who feels supreme loyalty toward a nation and places the highest importance on promoting national culture and national interests

nomads: desert-living herders who move seasonally with their herds in search of pasture and water

oasis: a fertile place in the desert where underground water comes to the surface

Quran: the holy book of Islam. The writings of the book were set forth by the Prophet Muhammad starting in A.D. 610. Muslims believe that Allah (God) revealed these scriptures to Muhammad.

sanctions: trade restrictions that limit a country's imports and exports, imposed to try to control or persuade a country

sharia: Islamic holy law, based in part on the Quran

Shiite: one of the two major sects of Islam, including about 10 percent of all Muslims. Shiites believe that only descendants of Muhammad's daughter Fatima and her husband Ali are rightful caliphs (Islamic leaders).

Sunni: one of the two major Islamic sects, including about 90 percent of all Muslims. Sunnis follow Islamic leaders who are not chosen from Muhammad's direct relatives.

Glossary

"Background Note: Libya." *U.S. Department of State.* **December 2004.**
http://www.state.gov/r/pa/ei/bgn/5425.htm (January 20, 2005).
This website provides facts about Libya's people, history, government, economy, and more. Travel warnings at http://www.state.gov/travel/.

Central Intelligence Agency (CIA). "Libya." *The World Factbook,*
2004. December 2004.
http://www.cia.gov/cia/publications/factbook/geos/ly.html (January 20, 2005).
The CIA's World Factbook series provides statistics and basic information about Libya's geography, people, government, economy, and more.

Cockburn, Andrew. "Libya." *National Geographic,* **November 2000,**
2–31.
After thirty years of isolation, Qadhafi allowed *National Geographic* magazine to do a cover story on the long-hidden land of Libya. This article is illustrated with photos and a map.

Cutter, Charles H. *Africa 2004.* **Harpers Ferry, WV: Stryker-Post, 2004.**
The article on Libya in the annual volume of the World Today series provides a moderately detailed look at recent culture, politics, and economics of the country.

Diagram Group. *Peoples of North Africa.* **New York: Facts on File,**
1997.
This book presents the different cultures and traditions of the major ethnic groups of North Africa, including the Arabs, Berbers, and Tuareg of Libya.

Economist. **2005.**
http://economist.com (January 2005).
This weekly British magazine, available online or in print editions, provides in-depth coverage of Libya's economic and political news.

Ham, Anthony. *Libya.* **Melbourne, AUS: Lonely Planet, 2002.**
This guidebook offers all the information you need about traveling to and around Libya and what to see there. Maps and photographs, and notes on history, language, and culture are also included. Lonely Planet also has a website, http://www.lonelyplanet.com, which can be useful for planning trips.

Herodotus. *The Histories.* **Translated by Aubrey de Selincourt.**
Baltimore: Penguin Books, 1954.
Herodotus was a Greek historian in the fifth century B.C., who set out to record all the information he was able to collect about all of the then-known world. He includes legends, traveler's tales, and popular belief, which make his writing interesting and sometimes amusing reading. Book four of *The Histories* includes a large section on Libya.

Library of Congress, Federal Research Division. *Libya: A Country*
Study. **1987.**
http://lcweb2.loc.gov/frd/cs/lytoc.html (August 8, 2004).
This study presents the dominant social, political, economic, and military aspects of Libyan society.

Libya: News and Views. 2005.
http://www.libya1.com/ (March 15, 2005).
Condensed news articles concerning Libya from international sources including UPI, AP, Reuters, and Arabic News. Updated daily, this site has archives going back to 1997.

Marozzi, Justin. *South from Barbary: Along the Slave Routes of the Libyan Sahara.* London: HarperCollins, 2001.
A fascinating account of a 1,150-mile (1,851 km) journey on camel with desert guides, from the Mediterranean coast of Libya, once known as the Barbary Coast, to the oasis of Al-Kufrah, once a center of the Saharan caravan trade. Marozzi, a British journalist, blends little details, such as how to mount a camel, with a large sense of history.

The Middle East and North Africa 2003. London: Europa Publications Limited, 2002.
The long section on Libya in this annual publication covers Libya's recent history, geography, and culture, as well as provides a detailed look at the economy, politics, and government of the country. Statistics and sources are also included.

Population Reference Bureau. 2004.
http://www.prb.org (January 21, 2005).
The bureau offers current population figures, vital statistics, land area, and more. Special articles cover the environmental and health issues of each country, including Libya.

Rogerson, Barnaby. *A Traveller's History of North Africa.* Brooklyn: Interlink Books, 1998.
Covering Morocco, Tunisia, Libya, and Algeria—countries with shared, as well as individual, history—this book considers North Africa to be "an island surrounded by three seas, the Mediterranean, the Atlantic, and to the south by the sand seas of the Sahara." The complex cultural background of the region, with its many peoples and conquerors, is woven with a colorful cast of characters in this very readable history of prehistoric times to the late twentieth century. Maps, a timeline, list of rulers, and illustrations accompany the text.

Swift, Jeremy. *The Sahara.* Amsterdam: Time-Life Books, 1975.
A natural, scientific, and cultural history of the Sahara by an author who has done extensive field research in the Sahara, including living with Tuareg herders in the Sahara. The accompanying photographs of desert landscape are astonishing.

African Studies Center at the University of Pennsylvania. *Libya.*
http://www.sas.upenn.edu/African_Studies/Country_Specific/Libya.html
Excellent academic source for online resources related to Libya, including a link to a site where you can read a translated copy of *The Green Book.*

Ayoub, Abderrahman. *Umm El Madayan: An Islamic City through the Ages.* **Boston: Houghton Mifflin, 1994.**
Umm El Madayan, or the Mother of Cities, is a fictional city representing any of many cities on Libya's North African coast. Finely detailed pen drawings by Francesco Corni wonderfully illustrate the history, architectural growth, and cultural development of the city as it evolves from a hunting-gathering site, to a Phoenician colony, to a Roman, then Arab city, and so on, up till the dawn of the twenty-first century.

Find Out More about Libya
http://www.geocities.com/Athens/8744/mylinks1.htm
Connect to Qadhafi's official website, find out what the time and temperature in Tripoli is at the present moment, read about camels and other desert animals, and discover all sorts of online resources about Libya at this site.

Gottfried, Ted. *Libya: Desert Land in Conflict.* **Brookfield, CT: Millbrook Press, 1994.**
Though this book for young adults ends soon after the United Nations imposed sanctions on Libya, it is a useful presentation of the powerful forces that shaped modern Libya and Qadhafi's controversial rule.

Keith, Agnes Newton. *Children of Allah.* **Boston: Little, Brown and Co., 1966.**
The author is an American woman who lived for nine years in Tripoli with her husband, who was part of a United Nation's reforestation program in the newly independent country of Libya. This is an insightful and interesting memoir of her friendships, daily life, and travels in Libya.

Libya: Our Home
http://ourworld.compuserve.com/homepages/dr_ibrahim_ighneiwa/
The Libya: Our Home website provides links to comprehensive resources on Libya including history, cultures, maps, photographs, books, music, sports, and industry.

Libyana
http://www.libyana.org/
Libyana is a collective, volunteer effort of a group of Libyan women and men who are dedicated to their culture and heritage. Their website includes samples of Libyan poetry, art, and music.

Malcolm, Peter, and Elizabeth Losleben. *Libya.* **Tarrytown, NY: Marshall Cavendish, 2003.**
Part of the Cultures of the World series, this title covers the geography, history, government, economy, people, and culture of Libya. It includes photos, sidebars, and fast facts.

Further Reading and Websites

Ondaatje, Michael. *The English Patient*. New York: Alfred A. Knopf, 1992.

This complex novel, set in the era of World War II, centers on a badly wounded Saharan explorer who always carries *The Histories* of Herodotus. As the reader learns the mysterious patient's love story, the factual history (and romance) of the exploration of Libya's deserts is also revealed. This book was made into a movie that won Best Picture at the 1996 Academy Awards. It was filmed in the breathtaking desert of neighboring Tunisia.

Sanders, Renfield. *Libya*. Philadelphia: Chelsea House, 2000.

Part of the Major World Nations series, this book is illustrated with photos and maps, and surveys the geography, history, people, economy, and culture of Libya.

Stolz, Joelle. *The Shadows of Ghadames*. Translated by Catherine Temerson. New York: Delacorte Press, 2004.

This is a balanced and evocative novel for young readers about the hidden world of Muslim women. Malika is turning twelve—marriageable age—in the historic oasis city of Ghadames (also spelled Ghadamis), Libya, at the end of the nineteenth city. Like her merchant father, who travels with the caravans, she longs to travel beyond the loving yet confining world of women's lives. One night a wounded stranger comes to the door, and her world and his are expanded as he teaches her to read and write Arabic.

vgsbooks.com
http://www.vgsbooks.com

Visit vgsbooks.com, the home page of the Visual Geography Series®, which is updated regularly. You can get linked to all sorts of useful online information, including geographical, historical, demographic, cultural, and economic websites. The vgsbooks.com site is a great resource for late-breaking news and statistics.

Willis, Terri. *Libya*. New York: Children's Press, 1999.

Part of the Enchantment of the World series, this title describes the history, geography, economy, culture, people, and religion of Libya. It also includes maps, photos, and facts and figures.

Winget, Mary, and Habib Chalbi. *Cooking the North African Way*. Minneapolis: Lerner Publications Company, 2004.

The cuisines of North Africa—Morocco, Algeria, Tunisia, Libya, and Egypt— are featured in this cultural cookbook. Besides offering a wide sampling of recipes, this book looks at the different peoples, customs, religions, and foods of the area.

Captions for photos appearing on cover and chapter openers:

Cover: This Berber granary (building used to store grain) was built in the fourteenth century. It was in use until as recently as the 1950s.

pp. 4–5 Most of Libya is covered by desert. Oases like this one provide welcome relief from the harsh desert conditions.

pp. 8–9 A man herds his camel across the barren Sahara. Camels are specially adapted to desert environments. They can survive on little water and on the sparse food the desert provides.

pp. 20–21 Ancient petroglyphs (carvings on stone) have been found in caves in the Sahara. The art includes animals such as these giraffes, which are 10 feet (3 m) tall, and indicates that the area was once lush grassland that supported people and animals.

pp. 38–39 Men and women wearing various styles of Western and traditional dress walk through a street in Tripoli.

pp. 48–49 Tuareg men perform a traditional sword-fighting ritual.

pp. 58–59 An oil refinery turns raw petroleum into useful products such as oil and gasoline. A vast majority of Libya's export revenue is generated by the nation's oil industry.

Photo Acknowledgments
The images in this book are used with the permission of: © Jean-Léo Dugast/ Panos Pictures, pp. 4–5, 10, 44, 48–49, 54; XNR Productions, pp. 6, 11; © Michael Totten, pp. 8–9, 13, 23, 53; © NASA/CORBIS, p. 14; © Jane Sweeney/Art Directors, pp. 16 (top), 38–39, 43, 45, 46, 47, 52; © Betty A. Kubis/Root Resources, p. 16 (bottom); © Th-foto Werbung/Art Directors, pp. 18, 40, 41, 50; © age fotostock/Superstock, pp. 20–21; Library of Congress, p. 26 (LC-USZC4-2705); © Bettmann/CORBIS, p. 28; © AP/Wide World Photos, pp. 29, 35; © Genevieve Chauvel/Sygma/CORBIS, p. 32; © Alain Nogues/ CORBIS SYGMA, p. 33; © Reuters/CORBIS, p. 34 ; © Sven Torfinn/Panos Pictures, p. 42; © Caroline Penn/Panos Pictures, pp. 56, 61; © Jack Stanley/Art Directors, pp. 58–59; © Betty Crowell, p. 62; © Ramzi Musallam/Art Directors, p. 63; © Jehad Nga/CORBIS, p. 65; Audrius Tomonis—www. banknotes.com, p. 68; Laura Westlund, p. 69.

Cover photo: © Michael Nicholson/CORBIS. Back cover photo: NASA.